The Bible Healing Promise Book

Compiled by
Mike Fugett

Copyright © 2007 Compiled by Michael Fugett

The Bible Healing Promise Book
Compiled by Michael Fugett

Printed in the United States of America

ISBN 978-1-60266-212-4

All rights reserved solely by the author. The author guarantees all contents are original and do not infringe upon the legal rights of any other person or work. No part of this book may be reproduced in any form without the permission of the author. The views expressed in this book are not necessarily those of the publisher.

Unless otherwise indicated, Bible quotations are taken from NIV Study Bible. Copyright © 1985 by The Zondervan Corporation Grand Rapids, Michigan, The Holy Bible, New International Version, copyright © 1973, 1978, 1984 by International Bible Society.

Other translations used:

Holy Bible — (NL) New Living Translation, Copyright © 1996 by Tyndale Charitable Trust — Tyndale House Publishers.

(ESV) English Standard Version, The Holy Bible, Copyright © 2001 by Crossway Bibles, A Division of Good News Publishers.

(NKJ) The New King James Version, Copyright © 1984 by Thomas Nelson Publishers.

(CE) The Holy Bible — Contemporary English Version, Copyright © 1995 by American Bible Society.

(AMP) The Amplified Bible, Expanded Edition, Copyright © 1987 by Zondervan Corporation and The Lockman Foundation.

CONTENTS

Foreword: by LeRoy Metzger	7
A Healing Prayer for You	9
Part 1: Your Healed Body	10
1. Healing for All Sickness and Disease	11
2. You Are Promised Good Health	17
3. Good Health Comes Freely With Salvation Through Faith in Jesus Christ	19
4. Strength to Equal Your Days	23
5. Healed and Restored Limbs	29
6. Bones, Bone Disease and Arthritis Healed	31
7. The Crippled, Paralyzed and Lame Healed	32
8. Well Rested and Peaceful Sweet Sleep	35
9. God Promises You Children	39
10. Healthy and Fruitful Womb	42
11. Healthy Child Birth	44
12. Eyes Healed	45
13. The Deaf and Mute Healed	47
14. Healthy Skin	49

15.	Healing Heart Disease	51
16.	Food Allergies Healed	52
17.	Well-Nourished Bodies	54
18.	Pain and Suffering Free	56
19.	You Are Protected From Sickness and Harm	62
20.	The Promise of a Long Life	70
21.	How to Live a Long Life	72
22.	Delivered From a Death Bed	75
23.	God's Abundant Healing Mercy and Grace	78
24.	Delivered and Set Free From All Addictions	82
25.	Rescued From Bad Medical Reports, Unfavorable Medical Diagnosis and Sickness Symptoms	86
26.	The True Revelation of Communion – Take Communion for Your Healing	89

Part 2: How to Pray For Healing — 98

27.	When You Pray for Healing – Believe You Received it and You Will Be Healed.	99
28.	Persevere in Prayer and Faith for Healing	107

Part 3: Scripture Principles for Healing — 111

| 29. | Get Healed Through Holy Living | 112 |

30.	Get Healed Through Giving	117
31.	Get Healed Through Praise, Worship and Thanksgiving	119
32.	Get Healed and Delivered From Demonic Affliction Through Praise and Worship	122
33.	Get Healed Through Godly, Healthy and Positive Thoughts	124
34.	Get Healed by Having a Godly, Healthy and Positive Confession	128

Part 4:	**Reasons You Can Be Confident For Healing**	**132**
35.	God Has a Healing Contract with You	133
36.	Jesus Loves to Answer Prayer for Healing	136
37.	Your Redemption from Sickness was Prophesied	141

Part 5:	**Spiritual Authority – Casting Out Demons**	**146**
38.	Authority in Christ for Victory Over Demonic Oppression and Attack	147
39.	Healed from Sickness and Conditions Caused by Evil Spirits	152
40.	You Will Heal the Sick and Drive Out Demons	155

Part 6:	**Healing the Inner Person**	**160**
41.	Healing for the Broken-Hearted	161

42.	Healing the Mind	**164**
43.	Break the Bonds of Stress and Anxiety and Walk in the Promise of Peace	**170**
44.	How to Live in Peace	**175**
45.	You've Been Set Free from Fear	**177**
46.	Live a Joy-Filled Life	**181**

Part 7: Healing The Spirit: Eternal Life — **185**

47.	Eternal Life Through Jesus Christ	**186**
48.	You Must Turn From Sin (Repent) to Receive Eternal Life	**189**
49.	Steps to Salvation and Eternal Life	**191**

Part 8: Major Obstacles to Receiving Healing — **194**

50.	Lack of Faith Will Hinder and Prevent Healing and the Miraculous	**195**
51.	Sin and a Lifestyle of Disobedience Will Hinder and Prevent Healing, and Bring On Sickness and Demonic Oppression	**199**
52.	Ungodly, Negative Thoughts and Attitude Can Produce a Sick and Oppressed Life	**206**
53.	Unforgiveness Will Hinder and Prevent Healing, Invite Sickness and Open the Door to Demonic Oppression	**209**
54.	Cursing Yourself with Sickness Through Word Curses	**213**

FOREWORD

1) Realize what you are reading - God's Living Word for you. The Word of God taken properly can bring healing to your *spirit, soul* and *body*. The Bible says God's Word is alive and powerful. Read the verse slowly and carefully and then read it again. Allow it to penetrate your whole body.

"For the Word that God speaks is *alive* and *full of power* [making it active, operative, energizing, and effective]; it is sharper than any two-edged sword, penetrating to the dividing line of the breath of life (soul) and [the immortal] spirit, and of joints and marrow [of the deepest parts of our nature], exposing *and* sifting and analyzing *and* judging the very thought and purposes of the heart". Hebrews 4:12 (AMP)

2) Pray the Word. When you're reading the Scripture and a particular verse speaks to you, stop and pray through it. Agree with it, personalize it and add your name to it. Take it as your own by faith, thanking God for it and submit it to memory.

3) **"Faith comes by hearing and hearing by the Word of God".** (Romans 10:17 NKJ) As you read and pray the Word of God, make it your confession of faith and speak it out loud; faith will begin to rise in your heart. Listen to this verse from the Apostle Paul and what he says about faith. **"Now FAITH is the assurance, (the substance, the confirmation, the title deed) of the things we hope for, being the proof of things we do not see and the conviction of their reality (faith perceiving as real what is not revealed to the senses)".**
- Hebrews 11:1 (AMP)

FOREWORD

What is faith? Faith is established conviction concerning things unseen and settled expectation of now and future blessing. The Greek word for substance literally means "a standing under," and was used in the technical sense of "title deed." The root idea is that of standing under the claim to the property to support its validity.

Thus, **"faith is the <u>title deed</u> of things hoped for"**. Assurance rests on God's Promises. And His Promises are greater and more powerful than any crisis or problem we face on earth. Why am I saying all this about faith? Because when you take *faith* and mix it with the *Word of God* you are getting all you can out of the healing promises of God. Listen to this final word about faith and the Word of God.

"For we also have had the gospel preached to us, just as they did; but the message they heard was of no value to them because those who heard did not combine it with faith".
- Hebrews 4:2

Just hearing the Word is not enough; it must also be believed, received and acted upon.

LeRoy Metzger,
Missionary to Malawi, Africa

A Healing Prayer For You

Almighty God, by faith in the Name of Jesus and through His shed blood; I boldly and in confidence approach Your Throne of Grace. I believe you hear me as I ask for and seek your healing power that will assuredly heal me. I know that by the wounds, bruises and beating on the body of Jesus' I have been healed from every sickness and disease. I claim Your Promise that You have forgiven all my sins and healed all my diseases. In full-faith and assurance I stand on Your promises of healing and receive them as mine by ownership. I praise You; I worship You and thank You for healing me, in the Name of Jesus. Amen.

References: Acts 3:16, Revelation 12:11, Hebrews 4:11, 1 John 3:21, 1 John 5:15, Matthew 7:7, Isaiah 53:4-5, 1 Peter 2:24, Matthew 8:17, 2 Corinthians 1:20, Psalm 103:2-4, Mark 11:23-24,

---

Dear Friends,

It is my prayer and heart's desire that as you pray and feed on these Scriptures and seek God for your healing, that you will be healed and restored completely. Proclaim what the LORD has done, to the Glory God. Praise the LORD.

God bless you,

Mike Fugett

PART 1
Your Healed Body

My son, pay attention to what I say; listen closely to My words. Do not let them out of your sight, keep them within your heart; for they are life to those who find them and health to a man's whole body.
- Proverbs 4:20-22

"All of these stones are the treasures of salvation. You are now touching the heavenly realm, and that one is the restoration of Life."
- *The Final Quest* by Rick Joyner

1
Healing for Every Sickness and Disease

"It's significant that the first Covenant promise (Exodus 15:26) God made with His people after crossing the Red Sea was the promise of healing. It was also at this time that God revealed Himself to Israel as their Physician. Through the redemptive and covenant Name of JEHOVAH-RAPHA [which is translated as "The Lord who heals you" or "The Lord your Physician"], God pledged to meet all of Israel's needs as they loved and obeyed Him."
- *God's Covenant of Healing* by S.J. Hill

Exodus 15:26
He said, "If you listen carefully to the voice of the Lord your God and do what is right in His eyes, if you pay attention to His commands and keep all His decrees, I will not bring on you any of the diseases I brought on the Egyptians, for **I am the LORD, who heals you**."

Note by F.F. Bosworth: "He cannot keep His Covenant without taking away our sickness and fulfilling the number of our days, according to His promise." – *Christ The Healer*

Exodus 23:25
Worship the Lord your God, and His blessing will be on your food and water. **I will take away sickness from among you**,

Deuteronomy 7:15
The LORD will keep you free from every disease. He will not inflict on you the horrible diseases you knew in Egypt, but He will inflict them on all who hate you.

2 Kings 20:5
Go back and tell Hezekiah, the leader of my people, this is what the LORD, the God of your father David, says: **I have**

Healing For Every Sickness and Disease

heard your prayer and seen your tears; I will heal you. On the third day from now you will go up to the temple of the LORD.

Psalm 19:7a (AMP)
The law of the Lord is perfect, restoring the [whole] person;

Author's Note: Meditate on God's word; it's the "perfect" medicine for restoring the "whole person" (spirit, soul and body).

Psalm 30:2
O LORD my God, I called to You for help and **You healed me**.

Psalm 41:3
The LORD will sustain him on his sickbed and restore him from his bed of illness.

Psalm 91:2-3
I will say of the LORD, "He is my refuge and my fortress, my God, in whom I trust." Surely He will **save you from the fowler's snare and from the deadly pestilence**.

Psalm 103:2-4
Praise the LORD, O my soul, and forget not all His benefits - Who forgives all your sins and **heals all your diseases**, Who redeems your life from the pit and crowns you with love and compassion,

Psalm 107:20
He sent forth His Word and healed them; He rescued them from the grave.

Isaiah 19:22b
They will turn to the Lord, and He will respond to their pleas and heal them.

Healing For Every Sickness and Disease

Isaiah 53:4
Surely He *(Jesus)* took up our infirmities and carried our sorrows (pains and suffering), yet we considered Him stricken by God, smitten by Him, and afflicted.

Author's Note: "Sorrows" - the Hebrew word used here is "mak'ob" and when translated means: pain, suffering and woes.

Isaiah 57:18-19
"I have seen his ways, but I will heal him; I will guide him and restore comfort to him, creating praise on the lips of the mourners in Israel. Peace, peace, to those far and near," says the LORD." "And **I will heal them**."

Jeremiah 30:12, 17
This is what the Lord says: "Your wound is incurable, your injury beyond healing. ... **But I will restore you to health and heal your wounds**," declares the Lord, "because you are called an outcast, for whom no one cares."

Jeremiah 33:6
"'Nevertheless, I will bring health and healing to it; **I will heal My people** and will let them enjoy abundant peace and security.'"

Matthew 4:23-24
Jesus went throughout Galilee, teaching in their synagogues, preaching the good news of the kingdom, and **healing every disease and sickness among the people**. News about Him spread all over Syria, and people brought to Him all who were ill with various diseases, those suffering severe pain, the demon-possessed, those having seizures, and the paralyzed, and **He healed them**.

Healing For Every Sickness and Disease

Matthew 8:16-17
When evening came, many who were demon-possessed were brought to Him, and He drove out the spirits with a word and **healed all the sick**. This was to fulfill what was spoken through the prophet Isaiah: "**He took** *(past tense)* **up our infirmities** *(past tense)* **and carried our diseases**."

Note by F.F. Bosworth: "When God puts a promise in past tense, He thus authorizes and expects us to do the same. Nothing short of this is appropriating faith." - *Christ The Healer*

Matthew 9:35
Jesus went through all the towns and villages, teaching in their synagogues, preaching the good news of the kingdom and **healing every disease and sickness**.

Matthew 11:4-5
Jesus replied, "Go back and report to John what you hear and see: The blind receive sight, the lame walk, those who have leprosy are cured, the deaf hear, the dead are raised, and the good news is preached to the poor."

Matthew 14:14
When Jesus landed and saw a large crowd, **He had compassion on them and healed their sick**.

Author's Note: Jesus is the same compassionate healer yesterday, today and forever. – Hebrews 13:8

Luke 4:40
When the sun was setting, the people brought to Jesus all who had various kinds of sickness, and laying His hands on **each one, He healed** them.

Luke 9:11
…He welcomed them and spoke to them about the kingdom

Healing For Every Sickness and Disease

of God, and **healed those who needed healing**.

Luke 13:12
When Jesus saw her, He called her forward and said to her, **"Woman you are set free from your infirmity."**

Acts 9:34
"Aeneas," Peter said to him, "**Jesus Christ heals you**. Get up and take care of your mat." Immediately Aeneas got up.

Acts 10:38
how God anointed Jesus of Nazareth with the Holy Spirit and power, and how He went around doing good and **healing all who were under the power of the devil**, because God was with Him.

2 Corinthians 8:9
For we know the grace of our Lord Jesus Christ, that though He was rich, yet for your sakes He became poor *(sin, sickness, and disease on the cross)*, so that you through His poverty might become rich *(healed and delivered)*.

Galatians 3:13
Christ redeemed us from the curse *(all sickness and diseases)* of the law by becoming a curse for us, for it is written: "Cursed is everyone who is hung on a tree."

Note by S.J. Hill: "Here it is plainly stated that on the cross Jesus Christ bore the curse of the law (Deuteronomy 28:21-22) and, therefore, has legally redeemed us from sickness and disease. Healing is not merely an incidental aspect of salvation of man, but is, in fact, an essential part of Redemption. Whoever embraces salvation by faith in Jesus Christ should recognize that the promise applies as much to physical health as it does to spiritual health." - *God's Covenant of Healing*.

Healing For Every Sickness and Disease

Colossians 2:9-10
For in Christ all the fullness of the Deity lives in bodily form, and **you have been given fullness in Christ**, Who is the head over every power and authority.

Author's Note: You have been given full physical Redemption and Atonement that covers any sickness and disease for life. - Isaiah 53:4-5

Hebrews 13:8
Jesus Christ is the same yesterday and today and forever.

Author's Note: Jesus Christ still heals today and forever.

1 Peter 2:24
He Himself bore our sins in His body on the tree, so that we might die to sins and live for righteousness; **by His wounds you have been healed**.

"If the fact that Jesus 'bore our sins in His body on the tree' be valid enough reason why we should trust Him now for the forgiveness of our sins, why is not fact that He 'bore our sicknesses' an equally valid reason why we should all trust Him now to heal our bodies?" – Unknown Writer

2 Peter 1:3
His divine power has given us everything *(healing)* **we need** for life and godliness through our knowledge of Him Who called us by His own glory and goodness.

Author's Note: "Everything" - the Greek word used here is "pas" and when translated means: all, everything, all things. **"Pas" includes healing**!

2
You Are Promised Good Health

1 Samuel 25:6
Long life to you! Good health to you and your household! And good health to all that is yours!

Psalm 35:27
May those who delight in my vindication shout for joy and gladness; may they always say, "The LORD be exalted, Who **delights in the well-being of His servant.**"

Psalm 139:14
I praise You because I am fearfully and wonderfully made; Your works are wonderful, I know that full well.

Psalm 144:12a
Our sons in their youth will be like well-nurtured plants

Proverbs 4:20-22
My son, pay attention to what I say; listen closely to My Words. Do not let them out of your sight, keep them within your heart; for they are life to those who **find** them and health to a man's whole body.

By F.F. Bosworth: "The Word of God cannot be health to either soul or body before it is heard, received, and attended to. Notice here the Words of God are life to those that "find" them. If you want to receive life and healing from God, take the time to find the Words of Scripture which promise these results." – *Christ The Healer*

Isaiah 33:24
No one living in Zion will say, "I am ill"; and the sins of those who dwell there will be forgiven.

You Are Promised Good Health

Isaiah 38:15-16
I will walk humbly all my years because of this anguish of my soul. Lord, by such things men live; and my spirit finds life in them too. **You restored me to health and let me live**.

3 John 1:2
Dear friend, **I pray that you may enjoy good health** and that all may go well with you, even as your soul is getting along well.

3
Good Health Comes Freely With Salvation Through Faith in Jesus Christ

Introduction by Author: There are two significant faith-building words in the New Testament that relate God's unwavering purpose and will for you to be healed and healthy: Saved and Salvation.

The word **"save"** or **"saved"** is translated from the Greek word "sozo" and it means: **healed**, cured, preserved, be made whole, and made well, deliverance from suffering and eternal salvation.

The word **"salvation"** is translated from the Greek word "soteria" and it means: **health**, healing, preservation, rescued, safety, deliverance from danger, and eternal salvation.

It's important that the meaning of these words, "saved" and "salvation," be comprehended and received deep in your spirit because they define the very heart of God towards healing the whole person. Hallelu Yah!

Consequently, the healing ministry of Christ and His work of eternal salvation are inseparable. (Isaiah 53:4-5, 1 Peter 2:24, Psalm 103:2-3)

Knowing that it is God's will for you to be healed is an essential truth that needs to be established in your heart for healing to come. Jesus said, "You will know the truth, and the truth will set you free." – John 8:32

John 3:17
"For God did not send His Son into the world to condemn the world, but to **save *(heal)*** the world through Him."

Good Health Comes Freely With Salvation Through Faith in Jesus Christ

John 10:9-10
"I am the gate; whoever enters through Me will be **saved *(healed)*.** He will come in and go out and find pasture. The thief only comes to steal and kill and destroy; **I have come that you may have life, and have it to the full.**"

Acts 2:21
And everyone who calls on the Name of the Lord will be **saved *(made well)*.**

Acts 11:13-14
... 'Send to Joppa for Simon who is called Peter. He will bring you a message through which **you and all your household will be saved *(cured)*.**'

Romans 5:10
For if, when we were God's enemies, we were reconciled to Him through the death of His Son, **how much more, having been reconciled, shall we be saved *(healed)* through His life!**

Romans 6:23
For the wages of sin is death, but the gift of God *(salvation)* is eternal life (and healing) in Christ Jesus our Lord.

Author's Note: The two fold redemption we have in finished work of Christ at the cross, (forgiveness of sins and healing for our bodies) are inseparable in the salvation God provides through Christ. (Isaiah 53:4-5, 1 Peter 2:24, Psalm 103:3)

1Corinthians 1:21
For since in the wisdom of God the world through its wisdom did not know Him, God was pleased through the foolishness of what was preached ***to save (heal) those who believe.***

Good Health Comes Freely With Salvation Through Faith in Jesus Christ

Ephesians 2:8-9
For it is by grace **you have been saved *(healed)*, through faith** -- and this is not from yourselves, it is a gift of God - not by works, so that no one can boast.

Ephesians 6:17 (Wycliffe New Testament, published by Terrence P. Noble,)
And take ye the helmet of health (salvation), and the sword of the Ghost, that is, the Word of God.

Author's Note: Good health and God's promises (the sword of the Holy Ghost) are yours for the taking.

Acts 13:26
"Brothers, children of Abraham, and you God-fearing Gentiles, **it is to us that this message of salvation (*good health and healing*) has been sent**."

Romans 1:16
I am not ashamed of the gospel, because it **is the power of God for salvation (*good health*) of everyone who believes**; first for the Jew, then for the Gentile.

2 Corinthians 6:2
For He says, "In the time of my favor I heard you, and in the day of salvation I helped you." **I tell you, now is the time of God's favor, now is the day of salvation *(health and healing)*.**

1 Timothy 2:3-4
This is good, and pleases God our Savior, who **wants all men to be saved *(healed)*** and to come to the knowledge of the truth.

Author's Note: It is God's Will that all people be healed.

Good Health Comes Freely With Salvation Through Faith in Jesus Christ

Titus 2:11
For the grace of God that brings salvation *(good health)* has appeared to all men.

Hebrews 2:3b
This **salvation (*good-health gospel*), which was first announced by the Lord**, was confirmed to us by those who heard Him. **God also testified to it by signs, wonders and various miracles**, and gifts of the Holy Spirit distributed according to His will.

Hebrews 2:10
In bringing many sons to glory, it was fitting that God, from Whom and through Whom everything exists, should make the Author of their salvation *(good health)* perfect through suffering.

4
Strength to Equal Your Days

Exodus 15:2
The LORD is my strength and my song; He has become my salvation. He is my God, and I will praise Him, my father's God, and I will exalt Him.

Numbers 23:22
God brought them out of Egypt; they have the strength of a wild ox.

Author's Note: Praise the Lord! What a great promise! Jesus redeemed us and brought us out of the world and provided us with strength of a wild ox.

Deuteronomy 33:25
The bolts of your gates will be iron and bronze, and **your strength will equal your days**.

Author's Note: The Lord promised strength for your whole life.

Deuteronomy 34:7
Moses was a hundred and twenty years old when he died, yet his eyes were not weak **nor his strength gone**.

Author's Note: God does not show favoritism regarding His promises. Romans 2:11

Joshua 14:10-11
"Now then, just as the Lord promised, He has kept me alive… So here I am today Eighty-five years old! I am still as strong today as the day Moses sent me out; I'm just as vigorous to go to battle now as I was then.

Author's Note: Joshua was still as strong at 85 years old as he was at 45 years old. If Joshua received these promises, so can you.

Strength to Equal Your Days

1 Samuel 30:6
David was greatly distressed because the men were talking of stoning him; each one was bitter in spirit because of his sons and daughters. **But David found strength in the Lord his God**.

1 Chronicles 16:11
Look to the LORD and His strength; seek His face always.

1 Chronicles 29:12
Wealth and honor come from You; You are the ruler of all things. In Your hands are strength and power to exalt and give strength to all. Now, our God, we give You thanks, and praise Your glorious Name.

2 Chronicles 16:9
For the eyes of the Lord range throughout the earth to strengthen those whose hearts are fully committed to Him.

Job 17:9
Nevertheless, the righteous will hold to their ways, and those with clean hands **will grow stronger.**

Psalm 18:1
I love you, O Lord, my strength.

Psalm 18:32
It is God who arms me with strength and makes my way perfect.

Psalm 19:7a (NIRV)
The Law of the Lord is perfect. It gives us new strength.

Author's Note: Meditate on the Law and the healing Promises of God's Word; it's the perfect medicine for giving you new strength.

Strength to Equal Your Days

Psalm 28:6-7
Praise be to the LORD, for He has heard my cry for mercy. **The LORD is my strength** and my shield; my heart trusts in Him, and I am helped. My heart leaps for joy and I will give thanks to Him in song.

Psalm 29:11
The Lord gives strength to His people; He blesses His people with peace.

Psalm 84:7
They go from strength to strength, till each appears before God in Zion.

Psalm 86:16
Turn to me and have mercy on me; grant Your strength to Your servant and save the son of Your maidservant.

Psalm 89:19a
Once You spoke in a vision, to Your faithful people You said: "I have bestowed strength on a warrior"

Psalm 105:37 (NKJ)
He brought them out with silver and gold, and **there was none feeble** among the tribes.

Isaiah 33:2
O LORD, be gracious to us; we long for You. Be our strength every morning, our salvation in time of distress.

Isaiah 40:29
He gives **strength to the weary and increases the power of the weak**.

Strength to Equal Your Days

Isaiah 40:31
but those who hope in the LORD **will renew their strength**. They will soar on wings like eagles; **they will run and not grow weary, they will walk and not be faint**.

Isaiah 41:10
So do not fear, for I am with you; do not be dismayed, for I am your God. **I will strengthen you and help you; I will uphold you with My righteous right hand**.

Isaiah 45:5
I am the Lord, and there is no other; apart from Me there is no God. **I will strengthen you**, though you have not acknowledged My Name.

Isaiah 45:24a
"They will say of Me, 'In the Lord alone are righteousness and strength.'"

Isaiah 58:11
The LORD will guide you always; He will satisfy your needs in a sun-scorched land and will **strengthen your frame**. You will be like a well-watered garden, like a spring whose waters never fail.

Ezekiel 34:16a
I will search for the lost and bring back the strays. I will bind up the injured and strengthen the weak

Acts 3:16
By faith in the Name of Jesus, this man whom you see and know was made strong. It is Jesus' Name and the faith that comes through Him that has given this complete healing to him, as you can all see.

Strength to Equal Your Days

1 Corinthians 1:8
He will keep you strong to the end so that you will be blameless on the day of our Lord Jesus Christ.

2 Corinthians 12:9
But He *(Jesus)* said to me, "**My grace is sufficient for you, for My power is made perfect in weakness.**" Therefore I will boast all the more gladly about my weaknesses, so that Christ's power will rest on me.

2 Corinthians 12:10
That is why, for Christ's sake, I delight in weaknesses, in insults, in hardships, in persecutions, in difficulties. **For when I am weak, then I am strong**.

Philippians 4:13
I can do everything through Him who gives me strength.

Colossians 1:17
He is before all things, and in Him **all things** hold together.

Author's Note: In Jesus, your physical body will "hold together."

1 Timothy 1:12
I thank Christ Jesus our Lord, Who has given me strength, that He considered me faithful, appointing me to His service.

2 Timothy 4:17
But the Lord stood at my side and gave me strength

Strength to Equal Your Days

Hebrews 11:32-34
David, Samuel and the prophets who through faith conquered kingdoms, administered justice, and gained what was promised; who shut the mouths of lions, quenched the fury of the flames, and escaped the edge of the sword; **whose weakness was turned to strength**.

1 Peter 5:10
And the God of all grace, who called you to His eternal glory in Christ, after you have suffered a little while, **will Himself restore you and make you strong**, firm and steadfast.

5
Healed and Restored Limbs

Genesis 49:24 (AMP)
But his bow remained strong *and* steady *and* rested in the Strength that does not fail him, **for the arms of his hands were made strong *and* active by the hands of the Mighty God of Jacob**, by the Name of the Shepard, the Rock of Israel.

1 Kings 13:6
…the man of God interceded with the Lord, and the king's hand was restored and became as it was before.

Nehemiah 9:21
For forty years You sustained them in the desert; they lacked nothing, their clothes did not wear out **nor did their feet become swollen**.

Psalm 18:33
He makes my feet like that of a deer; **He enables me to stand** on the heights.

Psalm 18:34
He trains my hands for battle; my arms can bend a bow of bronze.

Psalm 116:8-9
For you, O Lord, have delivered my soul from death, my eyes from tears, **my feet from stumbling, that I may walk** before the Lord in the land of the living.

Proverbs 31:17
She sets about her work vigorously; **her arms are strong for her tasks**.

Healed and Restored Limbs

Habakkuk 3:19
The Sovereign LORD is my strength; He makes my feet like the feet of a deer, He enables me to go on the heights.

Luke 6:6-10
On another Sabbath He went into the synagogue and was teaching, and a man was there whose right hand was shriveled ... He *(Jesus)* looked around at them all, and said to the man, "Stretch out your hand." He did so, and **his hand was completely restored**.

Author's Note: Jesus Christ is still healing shriveled hands today. Hallelu Yah! – Hebrews 13:8

Acts 3:6-8
Then Peter said, "Silver or gold I do not have, but what I have I give you. **In the Name of Jesus Christ of Nazareth, walk**." Taking him by the right hand, he helped him up, and instantly **the man's feet and ankles became strong**. He jumped to his feet and began to walk. Then he went with them into the temple courts, **walking and jumping, and praising God**.

6
Bones, Bone Disease and Arthritis Healed

Psalm 34:19-20
A righteous man may have many troubles; but the Lord delivers him from them all; **He protects all his bones**, not one of them is broken.

Proverbs 15:30
A cheerful look brings joy to the heart and **good news gives health to the bones**.

Author's Note: The good news is God's Word and salvation (eternal life and physical healing) through Jesus Christ. Meditate and believe on healing Scripture. This will bring good health to your bones.

Proverbs 16:24
Pleasant words are a honeycomb, sweet to the soul and healing to the bones.

Proverbs 3:7-8
Do not be wise in your own eyes; fear the Lord and shun evil. This will bring health to your bodies and **nourishment to your bones**.

Ezekiel 37:4-5
Then He said to me, "Prophesy to these bones and say to them, 'Dry bones, hear the Word of the Lord! **This is what the Sovereign Lord says to these bones: I will make breath enter you, and you will come to life**.

7
The Crippled, Paralyzed and Lame Healed

Proverbs 4:12
When you walk, your steps will not be hampered; when you run, you will not stumble.

Isaiah 35:4-6
say to those with fearful hearts, "Be strong, do not fear; your God will come, He will come with vengeance; with divine retribution He will come to save you." Then will the eyes of the blind be opened and the ears of the deaf unstopped. Then will **the lame leap like a deer**, and the mute tongue shout for joy. Water will gush forth in the wilderness and streams in the desert."

Isaiah 63:13
Who *(God)* led them through the depths? **Like a horse in open country, they did not stumble**;

Zechariah 10:12
"I will strengthen them in the Lord and **in My Name they will walk**," declares the Lord.

Malachi 4:2
But for you who revere My Name, the Sun of Righteousness will rise with healing in Its wings. And **you will go out and leap like calves released from the stall**.

Matthew 4:24
News about Him *(Jesus)* spread all over Syria, and people brought to Him all who were ill with various diseases, those suffering severe pain, the demon-possessed, those having seizures, and **the paralyzed, and He healed them**.

The Crippled, Paralyzed and Lame Healed

Matthew 8:6-7
"Lord," he said, "**my servant lies at home paralyzed and in terrible suffering.**" Jesus said to him, "**I will go and heal him.**"

Author's Note: Jesus is still healing the paralyzed because: "Jesus Christ is the same yesterday and today and forever." - Hebrews 13:6)

Matthew 9:5-6
"Which is easier: to say, 'Your sins are forgiven,' or to say, 'Get up and walk'? But so that you may know the Son of Man has authority on earth to forgive sins...." Then **He said to the paralytic, "Get up, take your mat and go home.**"

Matthew 11:4-5
Jesus replied, "Go back and report to John what you hear and see: The blind receive sight, **the lame walk**, those who have leprosy are cured, the deaf hear, the dead are raised, and the good news is preached to the poor."

Author's Note: The Lord has never stopped doing creative miracles. He has an infinite resource of new body parts that He still uses for making "the lame" whole.

Matthew 15:30
Great crowds came to Him, **bringing the lame**, the blind, **the crippled**, the mute and many others, and laid them at His feet; and **He healed them**.

Author's Note: Bring "The Lame," people that have missing or damaged body parts (feet, legs, arms, hands or any body part) come to Jesus (in prayer and faith) to receive the body part they need.

Matthew 21:14b
the lame came to Him *(Jesus)* at the temple, and He healed them.

The Crippled, Paralyzed and Lame Healed

Acts 4:9-10
If we are being called to account today for an act of kindness shown to a cripple and are asked how he was healed, then know this, you and all the people of Israel: **It is by the Name of Jesus Christ of Nazareth**, whom you crucified but whom God raised from the dead, **that this man stands before you healed**.

Acts 14:8-10
In Lystra there sat a man crippled in his feet, who was lame from birth and had never walked. He listened to Paul as he was speaking. **Paul looked directly at him, saw that he had faith to be healed and called out, "stand on your feet!" at that, the man jumped up and began to walk**.

Author's Note: "Faith comes from hearing the message." As the man listened to Paul speak about the full Redemption (forgiveness of sins and healing for the physical body) that Christ provided at Calvary. The lame man received the message by faith and was healed.

Romans 10:15
…As it is written: "How beautiful are the feet of those who bring good news!"

Author's Note: It is prophesied that if you tell ("bring good news") to anyone that Jesus Christ gives eternal life and heals broken bodies then your crippled, diseased or lame feet will be beautiful (healed).

Hebrews 12:12-13
Therefore, strengthen your feeble arms and your weak knees. "Make level paths for your feet," so that the lame may not be disabled, but rather healed.

8
Well Rested and Peaceful Sweet Sleep

Leviticus 26:6a
I will grant peace in the land, and you will lie down and no one will make you afraid.

Exodus 33:14
The Lord replied, "My presence will go with you, and **I will give you rest.**"

Deuteronomy 33:12
About Benjamin he said: "Let the beloved of the Lord rest secure in Him, for He shields him all day long, and **the one the Lord loves rests between His shoulders.**"

Joshua 1:13b
The LORD your God is giving you rest and has granted you this land.

Ruth 1:9a (NKJ)
The Lord grant that you may find rest, each in the house of her husband.

1 Samuel 26:12
So David took the spear and water jug near Saul's head, and they left. No one saw or knew about it, nor did anyone wake up. They were all sleeping, because **the LORD had put them into a deep sleep**.

1 Kings 8:56
"Praise be to the LORD, **who has given rest to His people Israel just as He promised**. Not one Word has failed of all the good Promises He gave through His servant Moses.

1 Chronicles 22:18a
He said to them, "Is not the LORD your God with you? And

Well Rested and Peaceful Sweet Sleep

has He not granted you **rest on every side**?

Job 11:18-19
You will be secure because there is hope; you will look about you and take your rest in safety. You will lie down, with no one to make you afraid and many will court your favor.

Psalm 3:5
I lie down and sleep; I wake again, because the LORD sustains me.

Psalm 4:8
I will lie down and sleep in peace, for You alone, O LORD, make me dwell in safety.

Psalm 16:8-9
I have set the Lord always before me. Because He is at my right hand, I will not be shaken. Therefore my heart is glad and my tongue rejoices; **my body also will rest secure**,

Psalm 23:2
He makes me lie down in green pastures; He leads me beside quite waters,

Psalm 91:1
He who dwells in the shelter of the Most High will **rest in the shadow of the Almighty**.

Psalm 127:2
In vain you rise early and stay up late, toiling for food to eat - for **He grants sleep to those He loves**.

Psalm 131:2
But **I have stilled and quieted my soul** *(mind)*; like a weaned child with its mother, like a weaned child is my soul within me.

Well Rested and Peaceful Sweet Sleep

Proverbs 3:24
When you lie down, you will not be afraid; **when you lie down your sleep will be sweet**.

Ecclesiastes 5:12
The sleep of a laborer is sweet, whether he eats little or much, but the abundance of a rich man permits him no sleep.

Isaiah 32:18
My people will live in peaceful dwelling places, in secure places, **in undisturbed places of rest**.

Isaiah 50:4
The Sovereign Lord has given me an instructed tongue, to know **the Word that sustains the weary**. He awakens me morning by morning, wakens my ear to listen like one being taught.

Isaiah 63:14
like cattle that go down to the plain, **they were given rest by the Spirit of the Lord**. This is how You guided Your people to make for Yourself a glorious Name.

Jeremiah 31:25-26
I will refresh the weary and satisfy the faint. At this I awoke and looked around. My sleep had been pleasant to me.

Matthew 8:24
Without warning, a furious storm came up on the lake, so that the waves swept over the boat. **But Jesus was sleeping**.

Author's Note: Jesus would also have us sleeping soundly through the furious storms in life. "Do not be anxious about anything." – Philippians 4:6

Well Rested and Peaceful Sweet Sleep

Mark 6:31
… He *(Jesus)* said to them, "**Come with Me by yourselves to a quite place and get some rest**."

Philippians 4:19
And my God will meet all your needs *(restful sleep)* according to His glorious riches in Christ Jesus.

Hebrews 4:1
Therefore, since the promise of entering His rest still stands, let us be careful that none of you be found to have fallen short of it.

Hebrews 4:9-10
There remains, then, a Sabbath-rest for the people of God; for anyone who enters God's rest also rests from his own work just as God did from His.

9
God Promises You Children

Genesis 1:27-28
So God created man in His own image, in the image of God He created Him; male and female He created them. God blessed them and said to them, "Be fruitful and increase in number; fill the earth...

Genesis 9:7
"As for you, be fruitful and increase in number; multiply upon the earth and increase upon it."

Genesis 20:17
Then Abraham prayed to God, and God healed Abimelech, his wife and his slave girls so that they could have children again,

Genesis 25:21
Isaac prayed to the LORD on behalf of his wife, because she was barren. **The LORD answered his prayer**, and his wife Rebekah became pregnant.

Leviticus 26:9
"I will look on you with favor and **make you fruitful and increase your numbers**, and I will keep my covenant with you."

Deuteronomy 7:13-14
He will love you and bless you and increase your numbers. **He will bless the fruit of your womb**... You will be blessed more than any other people; **none of your men or women will be childless**...

God Promises You Children

Judges 13:3
 The angel of the Lord appeared to her and said, "You are sterile and childless, but you are going to conceive and have a son."

Job 5:25
You will know that your children will be many, and your descendants like the grass of the earth.

Psalm 1:3
He is like a tree planted by streams of water, which yields fruit in season and whose leaf does not wither. **Whatever he does prospers**.

Psalm 92:14
They will bear fruit in old age, they will stay fresh and green.

Psalm 105:24
The Lord made His people very fruitful; He made them too numerous for their foes.

Psalm 107:41
But He lifted the needy out of their affliction and **increased their families like flocks**.

Psalm 115:14
May the Lord make you increase, both you and your children.

Psalm 127:3
Sons are a heritage from the Lord, children a reward from Him.

God Promises You Children

Psalm 128:1-3
Blessed are all who fear the LORD, who walk in His ways. You will eat the fruit of your labor; blessings and prosperity will be yours. **Your wife will be like a fruitful vine within your house; your sons will be like olive shoots around your table**.

Isaiah 44:3-4
I will pour out My Spirit on your offspring, and My blessing on your descendants. **They will spring up like grass in the meadow, like poplar trees by flowing streams**.

John 15:5
"I am the vine; you are the branches. If a man remains in Me and I am Him, **he will bear much fruit**; apart from Me you can do nothing."

Hebrews 6:13-15
When God made His promise to Abraham, since there was no one greater for Him to swear by, He swore by Himself, saying, "**I will surely bless you and give you many descendants**." And so after waiting patiently, Abraham received what was promised.

Hebrews 11:11
By faith Abraham, even though he was past age -and Sarah herself was barren -**was enabled to become a father because he considered Him faithful who made the promise**.

10
Healthy and Fruitful Womb

Author's Note: God has no favorites in whom He desires to have His promises fulfilled in. If Hagar, Sarah and Elizabeth received these promises, so can you.

Genesis 16:11
The angel of the Lord said to her: "You are now with child and you will have a son. You shall name him Ishmael *(God hears)*, for the Lord has heard your misery.

Genesis 18:13-14
Then the Lord said to Abraham, "Why did Sarah laugh and say, 'Will I really have a child, now that I am old?' **Is anything too hard for the LORD?** I will return to you at the appointed time next year and Sarah will have a son."

Exodus 23:26
And **none will miscarry or be barren in the land**. I will give you a full life span.

Deuteronomy 28:11a
The Lord will grant you abundant prosperity in the fruit of your womb

1 Samuel 1:27
I prayed for this child, and **the LORD has granted me what I asked of Him**.

1 Samuel 2:20-21
Eli would bless Elkanah and his wife, saying, "May the Lord give you children by this woman to take the place of the one she prayed for and gave to the Lord." Then they would go home. And the Lord was gracious to Hannah; she conceived and gave birth to three sons and two daughters.

Healthy and Fruitful Womb

2 Kings 4:16
"About this time next year," Elisha said, "you will hold a son in your arms."

Psalm 113:9
He settles the barren women in her home as a happy mother of children.

Luke 1:36-37
Even Elizabeth your relative is going to have a child in her old age, and she who is said to be barren is in her sixth month. **For nothing is impossible with God**.

Galatians 3:13
Christ redeemed us from the curse *(cursed and barren womb)* **of the law by becoming a curse for us**, for it is written: "Cursed is everyone who is hung on a tree."

Author's Note: Jesus Christ redeemed us from all curses, generational curses and curses of disobedience. The curse of disobedience in Deuteronomy 28:18 would bring a cursed and barren womb. Appropriate the above promise in Galatians 3:13, in faith, to your barren or childless womb for your healing. Jesus Christ redeemed you from it, He bore this curse on His body for you and it can't stay.

11
Healthy Child Birth

Exodus 23:26
and **none will miscarry** or be barren in your land. I will give you a full life span.

Psalm 139:14
I praise You because I am fearfully and wonderfully made; Your works are wonderful, I know that full well.

Isaiah 66:7
"Before she goes into labor, she gives birth; before the pains come upon her, she delivers a son."

Isaiah 66:9
"Do I bring to the moment of birth and not give delivery?" says the Lord. "Do I close up the womb when I bring to delivery?" Says your God

John 16:21
"A woman giving birth to a child has pain because her time has come; but **when her baby is born** she forgets the anguish because her joy that a baby is born into the world."

1 Timothy 2:15
But women will be saved *(sozo)* through childbearing--if they continue in faith, love and holiness with propriety.

Author's Note: The English word "saved" is translated from the Greek word "sozo" and it means: healed, cured, preserved, be made whole, made well, deliverance from suffering and eternal salvation.

12
Eyes Healed

Deuteronomy 34:7
Moses was a hundred and twenty years old when he died, **yet his eyes were not weak** nor his strength gone.

Author's Note: God does not show favoritism regarding His promises. Romans 2:11

Psalm 146:8
the LORD gives sight to the blind, the LORD lifts up those who are bowed down, the LORD loves the righteous.

Isaiah 29:18
In that day the deaf will hear the Words of the Scroll, and out of gloom and darkness **the eyes of the blind will see**.

Isaiah 42:6-7
"I the Lord, have called You *(Jesus)* in righteousness; I will take hold of Your hand. I will keep You and make You to be a covenant for the people and a light for the Gentiles, **to open eyes that are blind,** to free captives from prison and to release from the dungeon those who sit in darkness."

Author's Note: The Blood Covenant Christians have with Jesus includes opening the eyes of the blind. Hallelu Yah!

Matthew 9:28-29
When He had gone indoors, the blind men came to Him, and He asked them, "Do you believe that I am able to do this?" "Yes, Lord," they replied. Then He touched their eyes and said, "According to your faith will it be done to you";

Matthew 21:14
The blind and the lame came to Him *(Jesus)* at the temple, and He healed them.

Eyes Healed

Luke 7:22
So He replied to the messengers, "Go back and report to John what you have seen and heard: The **blind receive sight**, the lame walk, those who have leprosy are cured, the deaf hear, the dead are raised, and the good news is preached to the poor."

Author's Note: Jesus Christ is the same healer yesterday and today and forever. - Hebrews 13:6

Luke 18:40-42
Jesus stopped and ordered the man to be brought to Him. When he came near, Jesus asked him, "What do you want Me to do for you?" Lord, I want to see," he replied. Jesus said to him, "**Receive your sight; your faith has healed you**."

John 12:46
I have come into the world as a light, so that **no one who believes in Me should stay in darkness**.

Galatians 3:13
Christ redeemed us from the curse *(blindness and eye disease)* of the law by becoming a curse for us, for it is written: "Cursed is everyone who is hung on a tree."

Author's Note: Jesus Christ redeemed us from all curses, generational curses and curses of disobedience. The curse of disobedience in Deuteronomy 28:28 would bring blindness and eye disease. Appropriate the above promise in Galatians 3:13, in faith, to your eye disease or eye problem for your healing. Jesus Christ redeemed you from it, He bore this curse on His body for you and it can't stay. In Jesus Name.

13
The Deaf and Mute Healed

Isaiah 32:4
The mind of the rash will know and understand, **the stammering tongue will be fluent and clear**.

Isaiah 35:4-6
say to those with fearful hearts, "Be strong, do not fear; your God will come, He will come with vengeance; with divine retribution He will come to save you." Then will the eyes of the blind be opened and **the ears of the deaf unstopped**. Then will the lame leap like a deer, and **the mute tongue shout for joy**. Water will gush forth in the wilderness and streams in the desert.

Isaiah 42:18
"Hear you deaf; look you blind, and see!

Matthew 11:15
"He who has ears, let him hear."

Matthew 15:30
Great crowds came to Him, bringing the lame, the blind, the crippled, **the mute** and many others, and laid them at His feet; and **He healed them**.

Author's Note: Jesus heals the "The Lame." The lame, are people with missing or damaged body parts. Jesus makes no distinction between body parts. If you need eyes, ears, mouth, tongue, or any body part, come to Jesus (in prayer and faith) to receive the body part needed to be healed. Jesus can do anything! Hallelu Yah!

The Deaf and Mute Healed

Mark 7:32-35
There some people brought to Him a man who was deaf and could hardly talk, and they begged Him to place His hand on the man. After He took him aside, away from the crowd, Jesus put His fingers into the man's ears. Then He spit and touched the man's tongue. He looked up to heaven and with a deep sigh said to him, **"Ephphatha!"** (which means, "Be opened!") At this, the man's ears were opened, his tongue was loosened and he began to speak plainly.

Luke 4:18
The Spirit of the Lord is on Me, because He has anointed Me to preach good news to the poor. He has sent Me to proclaim freedom for the prisoners and **recovery of sight to the blind**, to release the oppressed

Luke 22:50-51
And one of them struck the servant of the high priest, cutting off his right ear. But Jesus answered, "No more of this!" And **He touched the man's ear and healed him**.

Author's Note: Jesus still replaces and heals damaged and missing body parts. "Jesus Christ is the same yesterday today and forever." - Hebrew 13:6

14
Healthy Skin

2 Kings 5:10-14
Elisha sent a messenger to say to him, "Go, wash yourself seven times in the Jordan, and your flesh will be restored and you will be cleansed." ... So he went down and dipped himself seven times, as the man of God had told him, and **his flesh was restored and became like that of a young boy**.

Job 33:24-25
to be gracious to him and say, 'Spare him from going down to the pit; **I have found ransom for him**' - then **his flesh is renewed like a child's**; it is restored as in the days of his youth.

Author's Note: Our ransom was Jesus. He suffered the wounds on His body, so that your "flesh is renewed like a child's."

Psalm 121:5-6
The Lord watches over you—the Lord is your shade at your right hand; **the sun will not harm you by day**, nor the moon by night.

Matthew 8:2-3 (NC)
Then a man with a skin disease came to Jesus. The man bowed down before Him and said, "Lord You can heal me if You will." Jesus reached out His hand and touched the man and said, "I will, be healed." And immediately **the man was healed from his disease**.

Matthew 11:4-5 (NC)
Jesus answered them, "Go tell John what you hear and see: the blind see, the crippled walk, and **people with skin disease are healed**.

Healthy Skin

Galatians 3:13
Christ redeemed us from the curse *(painful boils, skin diseases, festering sores, tumors and the itch)* **of the law by becoming a curse for us**, for it is written: "Cursed is everyone who is hung on a tree."

Author's Note: Jesus Christ redeemed us from all curses, generational curses and curses of disobedience. The curse of disobedience in Deuteronomy 28:35 would bring painful boils, skin diseases, festering sores, tumors and the itch. Appropriate the above promise in Galatians 3:13, in faith, to your skin disease or skin problem for your healing. Jesus Christ redeemed you from it, He bore this curse on His body for you and it can't stay. In Jesus Name.

Hebrews 13:8
Jesus Christ is the same yesterday and today and forever.

Author's Note: Jesus Christ still miraculously heals skin disease today.

15
Healing Heart Disease

Psalm 31:24 (NKJ)
Be of good courage, and He shall strengthen your heart, all you who hope in the Lord.

Psalm 73:26
My flesh and heart may fail, but **God is the strength of my heart** and my portion forever.

Isaiah 61:1
The Spirit of the Sovereign Lord is on Me, because the Lord has anointed Me (Jesus) to preach good news to the poor. **He has sent Me to bind up the broken hearted**, to proclaim freedom for the captives and release from darkness for the prisoners,

Ezekiel 36:26a
I will give you a new heart and put a new spirit in you;

1 Thessalonians 3:13
May the Lord strengthen your hearts so that you may be blameless and holy in the presence of our God and Father when our Lord Jesus comes with all His holy ones.

16
Food Allergies Healed

Leviticus 26:5
Your threshing will continue until grape harvest and the grape harvest will continue until planting, and you will eat all the food you want and live in safety in your land.

Exodus 23:25
Worship the Lord your God, and His blessing will be on your food and water. I will take away sickness from among you,

Psalm 147:14
He grants peace to your borders and **satisfies you with the finest of wheat**.

Author's Note: If you are allergic to wheat, this is your healing promise.

Proverbs 13:25
The righteous eat to their hearts' content, but the stomach of the wicked goes hungry.

Ecclesiastes 9:7
Go, eat your food with gladness, and drink your wine with a joyful heart, for it is now that God favors what you do.

Matthew 6:25a
Therefore I tell you, do not worry about your life, what you will eat or drink

Mark 6:42
They all ate and were satisfied,

Food Allergies Healed

1 Timothy 4:3-5
They forbid people to marry and order them to abstain from certain foods, which **God created to be received with thanksgiving by those who believe and who know the truth**. For everything God created is good, and nothing is to be rejected if it is received with thanksgiving, because **it is consecrated by the Word of God and prayer**.

17
Well-Nourished Bodies

Deuteronomy 11:15
I will provide grass in the fields for your cattle, and **you will eat and be satisfied**.

Nehemiah 9:20-21
You did not withhold Your manna from their mouths, and You gave them water for their thirst. For forty years You sustained them in the desert; **they lacked nothing,**

Nehemiah 9:25b
They ate to the full and were well-nourished; they reveled in Your great goodness.

Psalm 22:26
The poor will eat and be satisfied; they who seek the Lord will praise Him—may your hearts live forever.

Psalm 34:10
The lions may grow weak and hungry, but those who seek the Lord lack no good thing.

Psalm 37:19
In times of disaster they will not wither; in days of famine they will enjoy plenty.

Psalm 144:12
Then our sons in their youth will be like well-nurtured plants, and our daughters will be like pillars carved to adorn a palace.

Proverbs 3:7-8
Do not be wise in your own eyes; fear the Lord and shun evil. This will bring **health to your body and nourishment to your bones**.

Well-Nourished Bodies

Isaiah 27:2-3
In that day – "**Sing about** a fruitful vineyard. I, the LORD, watch over it; I water it continually. I guard it day and night so that no one may harm it."

Author's Note: The Lord calls us to "sing" – rejoicing – with a heart of gratitude – over what He is doing and what He has done.

Isaiah 58:11b
You will be like a well-watered garden, like a spring whose waters never fail.

Luke 1:53
He filled the hungry with good things but sent the rich away empty.

1 Corinthians 6:13b
The body is not meant for sexual immorality, but for the Lord, and **the Lord for the body**.

Author's Note: The Lord is all for taking care you physical body; keeping it well-nourished, strong and healthy.

Romans 8:11
And if the Spirit of Him Who raised Jesus from the dead is living in you, He Who raised Christ from the dead will also give life to your mortal *(physical)* bodies through His Spirit, who lives in you.

Ephesians 5:29-30
After all, no one ever hated his own body, but **he feeds it and cares for it, just as Christ does the church**--for we are members of His body.

18
Pain and Suffering Free

"If you're in need of healing, lay aside all un-scriptural teachings which encourage you to suffer physically with pain and sickness. Read the Father's will – His Word. Make use of His benefits in the Name of Jesus. Although Satan has blinded the hearts and minds of many from beholding all of the benefits of the cross, never lose sight of them, because God has not only forgiven you all your sins, but also healed you of all your diseases (Psalm 103:3)." – *God's Covenant of Healing by* S.J. Hill

Exodus 3:7-8
The Lord said, "I have indeed seen the misery of My people in Egypt. I have heard their crying because of their slave drivers, and **I am concerned about their suffering. So I have come down to rescue them** ..."

Exodus 3:17a
I have promised to bring you up **out of your misery.**

1 Chronicles 4:10
Jabez cried out to the God of Israel, "Oh, that You would bless me and enlarge my territory! **Let Your hand be with me, and keep me from harm so that I will be free from pain.**" And God granted his request.

Job 36:15
But to those who suffer **He delivers in their suffering**; He speaks to them in their affliction.

Author's Note: In the midst of waiting for the deliverance promise to be fulfilled, God promises He will speak to us – we will hear the voice of God. God will down load to us encouragement, revelation, direction, wisdom and truth.

Pain and Suffering Free

Psalm 22:24
For He has not despised or disdained the suffering of the afflicted one; He has not hidden His face from him but listened to his cry for help

Psalm 54:7
For He has delivered me from **all** my troubles...

Author's Note: "All" includes pain and suffering.

Psalm 69:29
I am in pain and distress; may Your salvation, O God, protect me.

Psalm 94:12-13
Blessed is the man you discipline, O Lord; the man You teach from Your law; You **grant him relief from days of trouble** *(pain and suffering)*, till a pit is dug for the wicked.

Author's Note: "Trouble" - the Hebrew word used here is "ra" and when translated means: pain, suffering, misery, soreness and affliction.

Psalm 107:6
Then they cried out to the Lord in their trouble *(misery)*, and **He delivered them from all their distress**.

Author's Note: "Trouble" - the Hebrew word used here is "sarl" and when translated means: misery, distress and anguished.

Psalm 107:41
But **He lifted the needy out of their affliction** *(suffering and misery)* and increased their families like flocks.

Author's Note: "Affliction" - the Hebrew word used here is "niy" and when translated means: affliction, suffering, misery and oppression.

Pain and Suffering Free

Psalm 118:5
In my anguish I cried to the LORD, and **He answered by setting me free**.

Psalm 119:45
I will walk about in freedom, for I have sought Your precepts.

Psalm 119:153
Look upon my suffering and deliver me, for I have not forgotten Your law *(promises)*.

Proverbs 11:21
But be sure of this: The wicked will not go unpunished, but **those who are righteous will go free** *(pain free)*.

Isaiah 14:3
The Lord gives you relief from suffering and turmoil and cruel bondage,

Isaiah 53:4-5
Surely He *(Jesus)* took up our infirmities and carried our sorrows (*pain and suffering*), yet we considered Him stricken by God, smitten by Him, and afflicted. But He was pierced for our transgressions, He was crushed for our iniquities; the punishment that brought us peace was upon Him, and **by His wounds we are healed**.

Author's Note: "Sorrows" - the Hebrew word used here is "mak'ob" and when translated means: pain, suffering and woes.

Pain and Suffering Free

Isaiah 53:10a
Yet it was the Lord's will to crush Him and cause Him to suffer,

Author's Note: At Calvary, God caused Jesus to suffer in His physical body for you. So that by His suffering *(for you)* in His body, you would not have to suffer in your body, for what He has already paid to suffer for.

Isaiah 58:6
"Is not this the kind of fasting I have chosen: to loose the chains of injustice and untie the cords of the yoke, to **set the oppressed free and break every yoke?**"

Isaiah 66:13
"**As a mother comforts her child, so will I comfort you**; and you will be comforted over Jerusalem."

Matthew 4:24
News about Him spread all over Syria, and people brought to Him all who were ill with various diseases, **those suffering severe pain**, the demon-possessed, those having seizures, and the paralyzed, and **He healed them**.

Author's Note: Jesus is still healing those suffering pain, "Jesus Christ is the same yesterday and today and forever."
- Hebrews 13:6

Matthew 8:6-7
"Lord," he said, my servant lies at home paralyzed and **in terrible suffering**." Jesus said to him, "**I will go and heal him**."

Mark 5:34
He said to her, "Daughter, **your faith has healed you. Go in peace and be freed from your suffering**."

Pain and Suffering Free

Luke 4:18
"The Spirit of the Lord is on Me, because he has anointed Me to preach good news to the poor. He has sent Me to proclaim freedom for the prisoners and recovery of sight to the blind, **to release the oppressed**,"

John 3:17
"For God did not send His Son into the world to condemn the world, but to **save *(sozo)* the world through Him**."

Author's Note: "Save" - the Greek word used here is "sozo" and when translated means: healed, **delivered from suffering**, and eternal salvation.

Acts 7:9-10
"Because the patriarchs were jealous of Joseph, they sold him as a slave into Egypt. But God was with him and **rescued him from all his troubles** *(suffering)*."

Author's Note: "Troubles" - the Greek word used here "thlipsis" and when translated means: trouble, suffering, anguish, hardships, distress, trials and afflictions.

Acts 7:34a
I have indeed seen the oppression of My people in Egypt. **I have heard their groaning and have come down to set them free**.

Acts 28:3-5
Paul gathered a pile of brushwood and, as he put it on the fire, a viper, driven out by the heat, fastened itself on his hand. ... But Paul shook the snake off into the fire and **suffered no ill effects**.

Pain and Suffering Free

Philippians 4:19
And my God will meet **all your needs according to His glorious riches in Christ Jesus**.

Author's Note: "All your needs" includes relief from pain and suffering.

1 Peter 5:10
And the God of all grace, who called you to His eternal glory in Christ, **after you have suffered a little while, will Himself restore you and make you strong, firm and steadfast**.

19
You Are Protected from Sickness and Harm

Exodus 12:23
When the Lord goes through the land to strike down the Egyptians, He will see the blood on the top and sides of the doorframe and will pass over that doorway, and **He will not permit the destroyer to enter your houses and strike you down**.

Author's Note: The New Covenant personal relationship we have with Father, the relationship that gives us free access to all His promises, is only made possible because Jesus Christ shed His blood to cover our sins. As the blood of Jesus covers our sins to make us pure and holy before Father, it also covers (protects and heals) our whole person: our spirit, soul (mind and emotions), and body. Father makes no distinction in what areas of our life He covers; He has guaranteed the blood of Jesus to cover **everything**.

Come to Father in prayer and ask Him to take the precious blood of Jesus Christ and cover your whole person (body and mind) with it. And ask Him to cover your spouse, children, relatives, home and everything you hold dear in your life. When we apply and are covered in the Blood of Jesus our enemy Satan is not permitted to strike us down. There is power in the blood of Jesus Christ!

We have overcome Satan by the blood of the Lamb and the word of our testimony. – Revelation 12:11

Exodus 23:20
"See **I am sending My angel ahead of you to guard you along the way** and to bring you to the place I have prepared."

Deuteronomy 7:15
The LORD will keep you free from every disease. He will not inflict on you the horrible diseases you knew in Egypt, but He will inflict them on all who hate you.

You Are Protected from Sickness and Harm

Deuteronomy 23:14
For the LORD your God moves about in your camp to protect you and to deliver your enemies to you. Your camp must be holy, so that He will not see among you anything indecent and turn away from you.

2 Kings 6:16-17
"Don't be afraid," the prophet answered. **"Those who are with us are more than those who are with them."** And Elisha prayed, "O Lord, open his eyes so he may see." Then the Lord opened the servant's eyes, and he looked and saw the hills full of horses and chariots of fire all around Elisha.

1 Chronicles 4:10
Jabez cried out to the God of Israel, "Oh that You would bless me and enlarge my territory! **Let Your hand be with me to keep me from all harm so that I will be free from pain.**" And God granted his request.

Job 5:19
From six calamities He will rescue you; in seven **no harm will befall you**.

Psalm 5:11
But let all who take refuge in You be glad; let them ever sing for joy. Spread Your protection over them, that those who love Your Name may rejoice in You.

Psalm 20:1
May the LORD answer you when you are in distress; may the Name of the God of Jacob protect you.

Psalm 28:7 (AMP)
The Lord is my Strength and my [impenetrable] Shield;
...

You Are Protected from Sickness and Harm

Psalm 32:6-7
Therefore let everyone who is godly pray to You while You may be found; surely when the mighty waters rise, they will not reach him. You are my hiding place; You will protect me from trouble and surround me with songs of deliverance.

Psalm 37:28
For the Lord loves the just and will not forsake His faithful ones. **They will be protected forever**, but the offspring of the wicked will be cut off;

Psalm 41:1-2
Blessed is he who has regard for the weak; the LORD delivers him in times of trouble. **The LORD will protect him and preserve his life**; He will bless him in the land and not surrender him to the desire of his foes.

Psalm 55:17-18a
Evening, morning and noon I cry out in distress, and He hears my voice. **He ransoms me unharmed from the battle waged against me…**

Psalm 57:1
Have mercy on me, O God, have mercy on me, for in You I take refuge. I will take refuge in the shadow of Your wings until disaster has passed.

Psalm 91:5-7
You will not fear the terror of night, nor the arrow that flies by day, nor the pestilence that stalks in the darkness, nor the plague that destroys at midday. A thousand may fall at your side, ten thousand at your right hand, **but it will not come near you.**

You Are Protected from Sickness and Harm

Psalm 91:9-12
If you make the Most High your dwelling - even the Lord, who is my refuge - then **no harm will befall you, no disaster will come near your tent**. For He will command His angels concerning you to guard you in all your ways; they will lift you up in their hands, so that you will not strike your foot against a stone.

Psalm 97:10
Let those who love the Lord hate evil, for **He guards the lives of His faithful ones**.

Psalm 105:15
"Do not touch My anointed ones; do My prophets no harm."

Psalm 121:6
the sun will not harm you by day, nor the moon by night.

Psalm 121:7
The Lord will keep you from all harm -He will watch over your life.

Psalm 140:7
O Sovereign Lord, **my strong deliverer, Who shields my head on the day of battle**.

Proverbs 1:33
But whoever listens to Me will **live in safety and be at ease, without fear of harm**."

Proverbs 12:21
No harm will befall the righteous, but the wicked have their fill of trouble.

You Are Protected from Sickness and Harm

Proverbs 18:10
The Name of the Lord is a strong tower; the righteous run to it and are safe.

Proverbs 29:25b
whoever trusts in the Lord is kept safe.

Proverbs 30:5
Every Word of the Lord is flawless; He is a shield to those who take refuge in Him.

Isaiah 43:2
When you pass through the waters, I will be with you; and when you pass through the rivers, they will not sweep over you. When you walk through the fire, you will not be burned; the flames will not set you ablaze.

Isaiah 52:12
But you will not leave in haste or go in flight; for the Lord will go before you, **the God of Israel will be your rear guard**.

Isaiah 54:17 AMP
But **no weapon that is formed against you shall prosper**, and every tongue that shall rise against you in judgment you shall show to be in the wrong. This [peace, righteousness, security, triumph over opposition] is the heritage of the servants of the Lord [those in whom the ideal Servant of the Lord is reproduced]; this is the righteousness or the vindication which they obtain from Me [this is that which I impart to them as their justification], says the Lord.

Isaiah 58:8b
Then your righteousness will go before you, **the glory of the Lord will be your rear guard**.

You Are Protected from Sickness and Harm

Isaiah 59:19 (NKJ)
So shall they fear the Name of the Lord from the west, and His glory from the rising of the sun; **when the enemy comes in like a flood, the Spirit of the Lord will lift up a standard against him**.

Jeremiah 29:11
"For I know the plans I have for you," declares the LORD, **"plans to prosper you and not harm you, plans to give you hope and a future."**

Daniel 3:26b-27
So Shadrach, Meshach and Abednego came out of the fire, and the satraps, prefects, governors and royal advisers crowded around them. They saw that the fire had not harmed their bodies, nor was a hair on their heads singed; their robes were not scorched, and there was no smell of fire on them.

Mark 16:18a
"they will pick up snakes with their hands; and **when they drink deadly poison, it will not hurt them at all**.

Luke 10:19
I have given you authority to trample on snakes and scorpions and to overcome all the power of the enemy; **nothing will harm you**.

John 17:11
…"Holy Father, **protect them by the power of Your Name - the Name You gave Me** *(Jesus)* - so that they may be one as We are One. While I was with them, I protected them and kept them safe by the Name You gave Me.

You Are Protected from Sickness and Harm

John 17:15
"My prayer is not that You take them out of the world but that you protect them from the evil one."

Acts 18:10
"For I am with you, and no one is going to attack and harm you"

Ephesians 6:16
Take up the shield of faith, with which you can extinguish all the flaming arrows of the evil one.

2 Thessalonians 3:3
But the Lord is faithful, and He will strengthen and protect you from the evil one.

Hebrews 1:14
Are not all angels ministering spirits sent to serve those who will inherit salvation?

Author's Note: If you are trusting Jesus Christ for eternal life, then you have angels serving and protecting you.

Hebrews 11:28
By faith he kept the Passover and the sprinkling of the blood, so that the destroyer of the firstborn would not touch the firstborn of Israel.

Author's Note: If the blood of an animal, applied in faith, protected God's people. How much more will the precious blood of Jesus when applied in prayer and faith - keep God's people safe! There is power in the blood of Jesus!

1 Peter 1:5
you who through faith **are shielded by God's power** until the coming of salvation that is ready to be revealed in the last time.

You Are Protected from Sickness and Harm

1 John 5:18
We know that anyone born of God does not continue to sin; the One who was born of God keeps him safe, and **the evil one cannot harm him**.

20
The Promise of a Long Life

Genesis 6:3
Then the LORD said, "My Spirit will not contend with man forever, for he is mortal; **his days will be a hundred and twenty years**."

Genesis 15:15
"You, however, will go to your fathers in peace and be buried at a **good old age**."

Deuteronomy 30:20
For the LORD is your life, and He will give you many years in the land He swore to give to your fathers, Abraham, Isaac and Jacob.

Ruth 4:15a
He will renew your life and sustain you in your old age.

Psalm 91:16
With long life will I satisfy him and show him my salvation."

Psalm 128:5-6
May the Lord bless you from Zion all the days of your life; may you see the prosperity of Jerusalem, **may you live to see your children's children**. Peace be upon Israel.

Isaiah 46:4
Even to your old age and gray hairs I am He, I am He who will sustain you. I have made you and I will carry you; I will sustain you and I will rescue you.

The Promise of a Long Life

John 10:10b
I have come that they may have life, and have it to the full.

Note by Wade Taylor: "This (Scripture) speaks of divine health and longevity of life. Those who receive this gift from Him will stand out from all others in the quality and length of their life span."
- *Longevity of Life*

21
How to Live a Long Life

Exodus 20:12
Honor your father and your mother; so that you may live long in the land the LORD your God is giving you.

Exodus 23:25-26
Worship the LORD your God ... and I will give you a full life span.

Deuteronomy 5:33
Walk in all the way that the LORD your God has commanded you, so that you may live and prosper and prolong your days in the land that you will possess.

Deuteronomy 22:6-7
If you come across a bird's nest beside the road, either in a tree or on the ground, and the mother is sitting on the young or on the eggs, do not take the mother with the young. You may take the young, but be sure to let the mother go, so that it may go well with you and you may have a long life.

Deuteronomy 25:15
You must have **accurate** and **honest** weights and measures, so that you may live long in the land the LORD your God is giving you.

Deuteronomy 32:46-47
He said to them, "Take to heart all the Words I have solemnly declared to you this day, so that you may command your children to obey carefully all the Words of this Law. They are not just idle Words for you - **they are your life**. By them you will live long in the land you are crossing the Jordan to possess."

How to Live a Long Life

1 Kings 3:14
And if you **walk in my ways and obey my statutes** and commands as David your father did, I will give you a long life."

Psalm 92:12 (AMP)
The **[uncompromisingly] righteous** shall flourish like the palm tree [be long-lived, stately, upright, useful, and fruitful]; they shall grow like a cedar in Lebanon [majestic, stable, durable, and incorruptible].

Proverbs 3:1-2
My son, do not forget My teaching, but keep My commands in your heart, for they will prolong your life many years and bring you prosperity.

Proverbs 9:11
For through Me your days will be many, and years will be added to your life.

Proverbs 10:27
The **fear of the LORD** adds length to life, but the years of the wicked are cut short.

Proverbs 28:16b
he who hates ill-gotten gain will enjoy a long life.

Habakkuk 2:4
the righteous will live by his faith

Authors Note: "The righteous will live (a long life) by his faith"

How to Live a Long Life

Matthew 4:4
Jesus answered, It is written: 'Man does not live on bread alone, but on every Word that comes from the mouth of God.

Author's Note: Live a long life by feeding on and standing on the promises of God.

John 6:53-57
Jesus said to them, "**I tell you the truth, unless you eat the flesh of the Son of Man and drink His blood, you have no life in you**. Whoever eats My flesh and drinks My blood has eternal life, and I will raise him up at the last day. For My flesh is real food and My blood is real drink. Whoever eats My flesh and drinks My blood remains in Me, and I in him. Just as the living Father sent Me and I live because of the Father, **so the one who feeds on Me will live because of Me**.

Author's Note: Jesus offers us divine health and long life when we - in faith, partake of communion. (See chapter 26: The True Revelation of Communion – Take Communion for Your Healing)

22
Delivered from a Death Bed

Judges 6:23
But the Lord said to him, "Peace! Do not be afraid. You are not going to die."

Psalm 33:18-19
But the eyes of the LORD are on those who fear Him, on those whose hope is in His unfailing love, to **deliver them from death** and keep them alive in famine.

Psalm 56:13
For You have delivered me from death and my feet from stumbling, that I may walk before God in the light of life.

Psalm 68:20
Our God is a God who saves; from the Sovereign Lord comes escape from death.

Psalm 72:13
He will take pity on the weak and needy and save the needy from death.

Psalm 102:19-20
The Lord looked down from His sanctuary from on high, from heaven He viewed the earth, to hear the groans of the prisoners and **release those condemned to death**.

Author's Note: He heals those on the death bed.

Psalm 118:17
I will not die but live, and will proclaim what the LORD has done.

Psalm 119:50
My comfort in my suffering is this: **Your Promise preserves my life**.

Delivered from a Death Bed

Proverbs 10:2
Ill-gotten treasures are of no value, but **righteousness delivers from death**.

Matthew 10:7-8
As you go, preach this message: The kingdom of heaven is near. Heal the sick, **raise the dead,** cleanse those who have leprosy, drive out demons. Freely you have received, freely give.

Matthew 11:5
Jesus replied, "Go back and report to John what you hear and see. The blind receive sight, the lame walk, those who have leprosy are cured, the deaf hear, **the dead are raised**, and the good news is preached to the poor."

Luke 7:14-15
Then He went up and touched the coffin, and those carrying it stood still. He said, "Young man, I say to you, get up!" The dead man sat up and began to talk, and Jesus gave him back to his mother.

John 4:49-50
The royal official said, "Sir, come down before my child dies." **Jesus replied, "You may go. Your son will live."** The man took Jesus at His Word and departed.

John 10:10
The thief comes only to steal and kill and destroy; **I have come that you may have life, and have it to the full**.

Delivered from a Death Bed

John 11:3-4
So the sisters sent word to Jesus, "Lord, the one You love is sick." When He heard this, Jesus said, "**This sickness will not end in death**. No, it is for God's glory so that God's Son may be glorified through it."

2 Corinthians 1:9-10
Indeed, in our hearts we felt the sentence of death. But this happened that we might not rely on ourselves but on God, Who raises the dead. He has **delivered us from such a deadly peril**, and He will deliver us. On Him we have set our hope that He will continue to deliver us,

Hebrews 11:33-35
through faith ... Women received back their dead, **raised to life again**.

23
God's Abundant Healing Mercy and Grace

1 Chronicles 16:34 (NKJ)
Oh, give thanks to the LORD, for *He is* good! For His mercy *endures* forever.

Psalm 23:6a (NKJ)
Surely goodness and mercy shall follow me all the days of my life;

Psalm 86:5 (NKJ)
For You, Lord, *are* good, and ready to forgive, and abundant in mercy to all those who call upon You.

Psalm 119:132
Turn to me and have mercy on me, as You always do to those who love Your Name.

Psalm 145:8 (NKJ)
The LORD *is* gracious and full of compassion, slow to anger and **great in mercy**.

Isaiah 30:18 (NKJ)
Therefore the LORD will wait, that He may be gracious to you; And therefore be exalted, that He may have mercy on you. For the LORD is a God of justice; Blessed are all those who wait for Him.

Isaiah 49:13 (NKJ)
Sing, O heavens! Be joyful, O earth! And break out in singing, O mountains! For the LORD has comforted His people, **and will have mercy on His afflicted**.

God's Abundant Healing Mercy and Grace

Lamentations 3:22-23 (NKJ)
Through the Lord's mercies we are not consumed, because His compassions fail not. **They are new every morning**; great is Your faithfulness.

Luke 1:50
His mercy *(healing mercy)* extended to those who fear Him, from generation to generation.

Luke 18:38-42
He called out, "Jesus, Son of David, have mercy on me!" Those who led the way rebuked him and told him to be quiet, but he shouted all the more, "Son of David, have mercy on me!" Jesus stopped and ordered the man to be brought to Him. When he came near, Jesus asked him, "What do you want Me to do for you?" "Lord, I want to see," he replied. Jesus said to him, "Receive your sight; your faith has healed you."

John 1:16
From the fullness of His grace we have all received one blessing *(healing)* after another.

Author's Note: Healing is apart of the fullness of His grace.

Romans 5:17
For if, by the trespass of one man, death reigned through one man, how much more will those **receive God's abundant provision of grace** and righteousness reign in life through the One man, Jesus Christ.

Author's Note: Receive God's abundant provision of healing grace.

God's Abundant Healing Mercy and Grace

Romans 8:32
He who did not spare His own Son, but gave Him up for us all -how will He not also, along with Him, **graciously give us all things** *(good health)*?

2 Corinthians 9:8
And God is able to make all grace abound to you, so that **in all things at all times, having all that you need**

Ephesians 1:7-8
In Him we have redemption through His blood, the forgiveness of sins, in accordance the **riches** *(healing riches)* **of God's grace** that He lavished on us with all wisdom and understanding.

Ephesians 2:4-5
But because of His great love for us, **God who is rich in mercy**, made us alive with Christ even when we were dead in transgressions – **it is by grace you have been saved** (healed).

1 Timothy 1:14
The grace of our Lord was poured out on me abundantly, along with the faith and love that are in Christ Jesus.

God's Abundant Healing Mercy and Grace

Titus 3:4-5a
But when the kindness and love of God our Savior appeared, He saved *(healed)* us, not because of righteous things we had done, but because of His mercy.

Author's Note: The English word "saved" is translated from the Greek word "sozo" and it means: healed, cured, preserved, be made whole, made well, deliverance from suffering and eternal salvation.

Hebrews 4:16
Let us then approach the throne of grace with confidence, so that we may receive mercy and find grace to help us in our time of need.

James 5:11
As you know, we consider blessed those who have persevered. You have heard of Job's perseverance and have seen what the Lord finally brought about. The Lord is full of compassion and mercy.

1 Peter 2:10
Once you were not a people, but now you are the people of God; once you had not received mercy, but now you have received mercy.

24
Delivered and Set Free From All Addictions

"It's insufficient to pray merely for strength to overcome temptation. We must go deeper than this and pray that every ungodly desire, which temptation feeds on, will be uprooted from our hearts. We also need to cry out for a love for God that will motivate us to overcome fleshly attitudes and passions." – *God's Covenant of Healing* by S.J. Hill

Leviticus 26:13
I am the LORD your God, Who brought you out of Egypt *(your addiction and sin)* so that you would no longer be slaves to the Egyptians *(your addiction)*; I broke the bars of your yoke *(addiction)* and enabled you to walk with heads held high.

2 Chronicles 20:17a
You will not have to fight this battle. Take up your positions; **stand firm and see the deliverance the Lord will give you**,

Psalm 34:17
The righteous cry out, and the Lord hears them; He delivers them from **all** their troubles *(addictions and cravings)*.

Psalm 37:39-40a
The salvation of the righteous comes from the Lord: He is their stronghold in times of trouble. **The Lord helps them and delivers them**;

Delivered and Set Free From All Addictions

Psalm 50:15
"and **call upon Me in the day of trouble; I will deliver you**, and you will honor Me."

Author's Note: Call upon the Lord in the day of addiction cravings; He will deliver you.

Psalm 72:12
For He will deliver the needy *(addicted)* **who cry out**, the afflicted who have no one to help.

Psalm 107:14
He brought them out of darkness and gloom and broke away their chains *(addictions)*.

Psalm 107:20
He sent His Word and healed them, and **delivered them from their destructions**.

Psalm 119:45
I will walk about in freedom, for I have sought out Your precepts.

Psalm 136:23-24
to the One who remembered us in our low estate - His love endures forever and **freed us from our enemies *(addictions)***, His love endures forever.

Psalm 142:7a
Set me free from my prison *(addiction)*, that I may praise Your Name.

Psalm 146:7
He upholds the cause of the oppressed and gives food to the hungry. **The LORD sets prisoners *(addicts)* free**,

Delivered and Set Free From All Addictions

Isaiah 49:8-9
This is what the Lord says: "to the captives, 'Come out,' and to those in darkness, 'Be free!"

Isaiah 61:1
The Spirit of the Sovereign Lord is on Me, because the Lord has anointed Me to preach good news to the poor. He has sent Me to bind up the broken hearted, **to proclaim freedom for the captives** *(addicts)* **and release from darkness for the prisoners**,

Matthew 6:13
"And lead us not into temptation, but **deliver us from the evil one** *(addictions, cravings and ungodly desires)*."

John 8:36
"So If the Son sets you free, **you will be free indeed**."

Romans 6:18
You have been set free from sin *(addiction)* and have become slaves to righteousness.

1 Corinthians 6:12
"Everything is permissible for me" – but not everything is beneficial. " Everything is permissible for me" – but **I will not be mastered by anything**.

Galatians 5:1
It is for freedom that Christ has set us free *(free from addiction and sin)*. Stand firm, then, and do not let yourselves be burdened again by a yoke of slavery (addiction).

Galatians 5:13
You, my brothers, were called to be free.

Delivered and Set Free From All Addictions

Colossians 1:13
For He has rescued us from the dominion of darkness *(addictions)* and brought us into the kingdom of the Son He loves.

Hebrews 2:18
Because He Himself suffered when He was tempted, He is able to help those who are being tempted.

1 Peter 2:24
He Himself bore our sins *(addictions)* in His body on the tree, so that we might die to sins *(addictions)* and live for righteousness; by His wounds you have been healed.

Revelations 1:5b
To Him who loves us and freed us from our sins *(addictions)* by His blood…

25
Rescued From Bad Medical Reports, Unfavorable Medical Diagnosis and Sickness Symptoms

"There is a higher level of truth then the facts. And that is God's truth. The real Truth is what He says about the situation."
- *An Integrated Approach To Biblical Healing* by Chester and Betsy Kystra

"Abraham's faith waxed strong while he looked unto the promises of God. Some people reverse this, and their faith waxes weak while they look at their symptoms, and forget the promise. Since God healed by sending His Word, which is the only basis for our faith, we will miss healing if we allow our symptoms to hinder us from expecting what His word promises." – *Christ The Healer* by F.F. Bosworth

"We are to think faith, speak faith, act faith, and keep it until the promise is fulfilled. By being occupied with symptoms or feelings, we violate the conditions and thereby turn off the switch to His power. Faith regards all contrary symptoms as "lying vanities" (Jonah 2:8 KJV) as Jonah did, and puts the Word in the place of the senses." By F. F. Bosworth

Exodus 14:13
Do not be afraid. Stand firm and **you will see the deliverance the Lord will bring you today**.

1 Samuel 10:19
Your God, who saves you **out of all your calamities** and distresses.

Psalm 41:1
Blessed is he who has regard for the weak; the Lord delivers him in times of trouble.

Rescued From Bad Medical Reports, Unfavorable Medical Diagnosis and Sickness Symptoms

Psalm 54:7
For He has delivered me from all my troubles, and my eyes have looked in triumph on my foes.

Psalm 91:14-15
"**Because he loves me**," says the LORD, "**I will rescue him; I will protect him**, for he acknowledges My Name. He will call upon Me, and I will answer him; **I will be with him in trouble, I will deliver him** and honor him.

Proverbs 11:8
A righteous man is rescued from trouble, and it comes on the wicked instead.

Jonah 2:8 (KJV)
They that observe lying vanities *(symptoms and circumstances)* forsake their own mercy.

Author's Note: The mighty man of faith Jonah gave the name "lying vanities" to the symptoms and circumstances that appeared to stand in his way from expecting God's mercy. Instead he trusted God and sacrificed and praised with a voice of thanksgiving while still in the stomach of the great fish and was delivered. Glory to God!!!

Zechariah 10:11
They will pass through the sea of trouble; the surging sea will be subdued

Rescued From Bad Medical Reports, Unfavorable Medical Diagnosis and Sickness Symptoms

Mark 5:35-36
While Jesus was still speaking, some men came from the house of Jairus, the synagogue ruler. "Your daughter is dead," they said. "Why bother the teacher any more?" Ignoring what they said, Jesus told the synagogue ruler, "Don't be afraid; just believe."

Author's Note: Whenever you hear a bad medical report like the "synagogue ruler" did, "ignore what they said," "don't be afraid; just believe" that Jesus will heal and deliver you.

2 Corinthians 1:10
He has delivered us from such a deadly peril, and **He will deliver us**. On Him we have set our hope that He will continue to deliver us,

Philippians 1:19
for I know that through your prayers and the help given by the Spirit of Jesus Christ, **what has happen to me will turn out for my deliverance**.

2 Timothy 4:18
The Lord will rescue me from every evil attack and will bring me safely to His heavenly kingdom. To Him be glory for ever and ever. Amen.

26
The True Revelation of Communion - Take Communion for Your Healing

Introduction by Author:

Spiritual healing came through the shed blood of Jesus for the forgiveness of our sins.

Physical healing came through the wounds He carried on His body (1 Peter 2:24, Isaiah 53:4-5).

When we participate and have a part in the "Lord's table," eating of the bread (which represents His body), we are receiving and participating in faith, believing, what He did for us on His body. ("the bread we eat is a participation in the body of Christ," - 1 Corinthians 10:16)

When we take the bread and say in our hearts or say out loud, in faith, "Lord I remember and receive what You received on your body, the full payment – full redemption, You paid with Your body to take away my sickness and diseases [verbally name your ailments]. Then we get an exchange and a transfer of the healing grace of Jesus through "participation in the body of Christ" during "The Lord's supper." The cross is the exchange. It is a full exchange. When you remember, acknowledge and receive His body (represented by the bread) and what it represents (your stomach cancer, arthritis, deafness, blindness, skin disease or whatever your sickness or disease), for your complete healing and restoration then Jesus takes your sickness and disease in exchange.

Note by A.J. Gordon: "Since our substitute bore our sins and sicknesses, did He not do so that we might not bare them?"

The True Revelation of Communion - Take Communion for Your Healing

Author's Note: When Jesus hung on the cross and said, "It is finished," He was saying the redemption of mankind [spirit, soul (mind/emotions) and physical body] is paid in full.

It is Satan's plan to cover up everything Jesus did at Calvary. At Calvary, Jesus was made to be sick for our sickness as He was made to be sin for our sins.
(2 Corinthians 5:21).

Don't miss out on this benefit! Get healed through taking communion, this is one of God's intended benefits for taking it. Precept upon precept the Scriptures reveal this wonderful truth:

The Foundation for True Communion

Luke 22:19
And He *(Jesus)* took bread, gave thanks and broke it, and gave it to them, saying, **"This is My body given for you** *(Isaiah 53:4-5)*; do this in remembrance of Me."

Author's Note: When you take and eat the bread it should put you in remembrance of how Jesus was horribly beaten, bruised and wounded. He suffered every kind of sickness and disease on His body to pay for your sins and you're healing. His sacrifice was paid for any affliction you might be suffering at the present time, and your need to remember and receive healing for what He sacrificed His body for.

When Jesus said, "This is My body given for you," He was in fact telling the church again that he was fulfilling the prophecy Isaiah made about Him 700 years before that. Isaiah prophesied that Jesus was coming to bring redemption. He was coming to bring spiritual, mental, emotion and physical redemption.

The True Revelation of Communion - Take Communion for Your Healing

Isaiah 53:4 (YLT)
Surely our **sicknesses** He hath borne, and our **pains** -- He hath carried them, and we -- we have esteemed Him plagued, Smitten of God, and afflicted.

Isaiah 53:5
But He was **pierced for our transgressions**; He was **crushed for our iniquities** *(for spiritual redemption)*; **the punishment that brought us peace was upon Him** (for mental, emotion and relational redemption), and **by His wounds we are healed** *(for physical redemption)*.

Isaiah 53:10
Yet it was the Lord's will to **crush** Him *(Jesus)* and cause him to **suffer**,

Hebrews 10:5 (NLV)
When Christ came into the world, He said to God, "You do not want animals killed or gifts given in worship. **You have made My body ready as a gift.**"

Author's Note: The "gift" was spiritual, emotional and physical redemption. It was the Father's will to have Jesus' body made ready (by suffering) as a gift to Him, so that His beloved mankind could be spiritually saved, bodily healed and live a long life.

Isaiah 50:6
I offered My back to those who **beat** me, My cheeks to those who pulled out My beard; I did not hide My face from mocking and spitting.

Author's Note: "With His stripes *("put on His back by those who beat Him")* we are healed." – Isaiah 53:5 (KJV) (physical redemption*)*

The True Revelation of Communion - Take Communion for Your Healing

1 Peter 2:24
by His **wounds** you have been healed.

Isaiah 52:14
Just as there were many who were appalled at Him —His appearance was so **disfigured** beyond that of any man and His form **marred** beyond human likeness—

Matthew 27:47
Jesus cried out in a loud voice ... "My God, my God, why have you **forsaken** Me?"

Author's Note: "Forsaken" for your spiritual, emotional rejection, relational and abandonment redemption.

Isaiah 53:11
After the **suffering of His soul**, He *(Jesus)* will see the light of life and be satisfied.

Author's Note: Jesus suffered for your mental and emotional redemption (deliverance and healing).

Zechariah 9:11
As for you, because of the blood of my (Yeshua the Messiah – Jesus Christ) covenant with you, I (Yeshua) will free your prisoners from (all sickness, disease, demonic oppression, emotional bondage, and eternal punishment)

Matthew 8:16-17
He healed all the sick. This was to fulfill what was spoken through the prophet Isaiah: "He took up our infirmities and carried our diseases."

The True Revelation of Communion - Take Communion for Your Healing

Hebrews 9:28
So as Christ was sacrificed once to take away the sins of many people,

Author's Note: Likewise, "Christ was sacrificed once to take away" sickness of many people.

Note by F.F. Bosworth: "The Lord's Supper is more than an ordinance, because we may partake of Christ while we are partaking of the emblems of His death and the benefits there of. In Christ there is both bodily and spiritual life, and surely there is no better time for availing ourselves of the privilege of having the "life also of Jesus . . . made manifest in our mortal flesh." (2 Corinthians 4:11) - *Christ The Healer*

Participation In Christ

Author's Note: The Apostle Paul said, "I am resolved to know nothing except Jesus Christ and Him crucified." (1 Corinthians 2:2) Paul was committed to living out and experiencing Christ's total Atonement and Redemption in every area of his life.

1 Corinthians 11:24 (YLT)
and having given thanks, He brake, and said, `Take ye, eat ye, this is My body, that for you is being broken; **this do ye -- to the remembrance of Me.**'

Author's Note: When we take and eat the bread, we are to remember that fact that Jesus took all sickness and diseases on His body (Matthew 8:17, 1 Peter 2:24), so that we can be healed and live a long life. The bread and the wine are only elements to remind us of what Jesus did for us spiritually and physically.

The True Revelation of Communion - Take Communion for Your Healing

John 6:32-33
it is My Father who gives you the true bread from heaven. For the bread of God is He who comes down from heaven and **gives life** to the world."

Definition by Vine's Expository Dictionary of Biblical Words: for the words "gives life" in John 6:33: "For the life that He gives He maintains."

Author's Note: Taking communion is the most intimate position we can get in Christ – taking His body in us. Jesus is the Living Word and when we take Him in us through communion it produces health and long life.

Those who take communion can walk in divine health. It is important to be single-minded on the benefits God has in the Atonement of not only forgiveness of sins but healing for all your diseases. You can not be double-minded if you want the benefits of the Atonement.

Note by F.F. Bosworth: "It is by realizing that our redemption from sickness was actually accomplished in the body of our crucified Lord, and by whole-heartedly believing and receiving what God declares in His written Word about the matter, that the Holy Spirit gives us the personal experience of Christ as our Physician."
– *Christ The Healer*

The Grace of Communion

1 Corinthians 11:27-31
Therefore, whoever eats the bread or drinks the cup of the Lord in an unworthy manner will be guilty of sinning against the body and the blood of the Lord. A man ought to **examine himself before he eats the bread and drinks of the cup**. For anyone who eats and drinks without recognizing the Body of the Lord eats and drinks judgment

The True Revelation of Communion - Take Communion for Your Healing

on himself. That is why many among you are weak and sick, and a number of you have fallen asleep. But if we judged ourselves, we would not come under judgment.

Author's Note: Paul said when you eat the bread in a worthy manner you won't remain weak, sick and die prematurely. When we put faith in receiving what Jesus did at Calvary – then we can walk in divine health.

Communion is a holy act and it gives glory to God (1 Corinthians 10:31). It will produce wonderful results or fearful results depending on how one takes it. Jesus paid a great price on His body to provide for your forgiveness of sins and healing.

So it's important that before you eat the bread or drink the cup, you should be very careful to <u>examine yourself</u>: Think and ask yourself, in very serious honesty, "What afflictions in my life need to be redeemed through the redemption Jesus' body bought for me?" Is it a emotional or physical need? Is there any sins or bad heart attitudes that you need to ask forgiveness for and get cleansed anew with the blood of Jesus? Whatever the need, He insists that you recognize it and participate in the redemption He paid for with His body. Jesus does not want you carrying around on your body an affliction or sin that He suffered for on His body to pay for you to walk in freedom from it.

Verse 31 says that judging ourselves, is a critical part of examining ourselves, prior to participating in the "Lord's Supper." We don't want to "be guilty of sinning against the body of the Lord." **The Promises of God are conditional as the consequences for disobedience are avoidable**. God says to judge (repent) and make right with God, any obstacles that would stop us from receiving the benefits of communion: disobedience, willful sins, un-confessed sins, double-mindedness, unworthiness, thoughts that your sickness is too small a thing or too big a thing to take before God for redemption, doubts and unbelief that the Atonement which Jesus paid on and in His body is sufficient enough to heal you.

The True Revelation of Communion - Take Communion for Your Healing

You Are Authorized To Take Communion

Author's Note: God has given the opportunity to all Christians to take communion everyday wherever we happen to be. We are all "ambassadors for Christ" and appointed "priests" and "ministers" unto God. So we don't have to wait to receive communion at church that is given by a priest or an ordained minister. If you are sick take communion everyday and at every meal and you will get healed. There can be a progressive healing or an instantaneous healing.

Revelation 5:10
You have made them to be a kingdom and priests to serve our God...

2 Corinthians 5:20
We are therefore Christ's ambassadors

2 Corinthians 3:6
He has made us competent as ministers of a new covenant

Author's Note: **"This is My body given for you; do this in remembrance of Me."** A communion service should be a healing service. We are to remember the wounds He bore on His body were for our physical healing. Receive His broken Body in exchange for your broken body. Take God at His Word. Eat the eye of Christ for your eyes. Eat the hip of Christ for your hip. Eat the brains of Christ for your mind. (John 6:53-57)

Take Communion Daily

Acts 2:46 (NLT)
They worshiped together at the temple each day, met in homes for the Lord's Supper, and shared their meals with great joy and generosity -

The True Revelation of Communion - Take Communion for Your Healing

Note by Wade Taylor: "Our eating food to sustain our natural body is not an option; rather it is a necessity. Also, our "partaking" of the life of the Lord is not an option. This partaking of the "body" and the "blood" of the Lord must take place more often than partaking of His life through communion on the first Sunday of each month. Rather, we must partake on a regular (daily) basis, or we will suffer loss, both spiritually and naturally. The Word says, "as often as you partake," communion can be taken as often as we desire. If we realize we are partaking of healing and life, we will take it often."

A True Communion Prayer

Father as I hold this bread up to You, I thank You for it. I ask that You would sanctify it as the body of Christ. That suffered and took on every sickness and disease for every part of my body. That fully redeemed me spiritually, mentally and physically. And as I partake of the body of Christ, I receive healing in every organ, in every cell and in every function in my body in Jesus Name.

Lord we thank You for this wine as representing the blood of Jesus which justified us in Your sight. We receive now the blood of Jesus in our life which cleanses us from all unrighteousness. The life of the flesh is in the blood, so Father we receive Your life right now anew in our bodies as we receive this wine in Jesus Name.

- Some thoughts expressed in this chapter were taken from: Sid Roth's Messianic Vision Radio Show interview, "Insights into Communion" with Dr. John Miller on April 7, 2003

PART 2
How to Pray For Healing

"I tell you the truth, if anyone says to this mountain, 'Go, throw yourself into the sea,' and does not doubt in his heart but believes that what he says will happen, it will be done for him. Therefore I tell you, whatever you ask for in prayer, believe that you have received it, and it will be yours."
- Mark 11:23-24

"In Mark 11:24, Jesus commands us to believe we "have received" the things we pray for, at the time we pray without waiting to see or feel them; and on this condition He promises, "*it will* be yours." Faith for healing of your body, the same as faith for forgiveness, is to believe, on the authority of God's Word, that you were forgiven before you felt forgiven. Nothing else is faith, for "Faith is being certain of what *we do not see*." As soon as the blessing we take by faith is *manifested*, faith for that blessing ends."
- *Christ The Healer* by F.F. Bosworth

27
When You Pray for Healing - Believe You Received it and You Will Be Healed

"Faith is expecting God to keep His promise. In fact, God's way of doing everything is by making promises and then fulfilling them wherever they produce faith.

Faith for healing is to receive the written healing promise of God as a direct message to you. His healing promise means the same as if He appeared to you and said, "I have heard your prayer.

Faith is the most rational thing in the world, because it is based on the greatest of facts and realities. It sees God; it sees Calvary where disease and sin were canceled. It sees the promises of God and His faithfulness, which is more certain than the foundations of a mountain. Faith sees the health and strength given on the cross as already belonging to us; it receives the words: "He took our infirmities and carried our diseases" (Matthew 8:17) and acts accordingly. What the eye of faith sees, the *hand* of faith appropriates, saying, "This is mine by virtue of the promise of God." Faith refuses to see anything but God and what He says."
- *Christ The Healer* by F.F. Bosworth

Psalm 18:25a
To the faithful You show Yourself faithful,

Psalm 27:13
I am still confident of this: **I will see the goodness *(healing)* of the Lord in the land of the living**.

Author's Note: The Lord wants us to be confident that we will receive healing.

When You Pray for Healing - Believe You Received it and You Will Be Healed

Psalm 28:7a (AMP)
The Lord is my Strength and my [impenetrable] Shield; **my heart trusts in, relies on, and confidently leans on Him, and I am helped (healed)**;

Daniel 6:23b
And when Daniel was lifted from the den, **no wound was found on him, because he trusted in his God**.

Habakkuk 2:4b
the righteous will live by his faith

Author's Note: "The righteous live *(live in health)* by his faith."

Matthew 8:6-8, 13
"Lord," he said, my servant lies at home paralyzed and in terrible suffering." Jesus said to him, "I will go and heal him." The centurion replied, "Lord, I do not deserve to have You come under my roof. But just say the word, and my servant will be healed. Then Jesus said to the centurion, "Go! **It will be done (healed) just as you believed it would**." And his servant was healed at that very hour.

Matthew 9:28-30
When He had gone indoors, the blind men came to Him, and He asked them, "**Do you believe that I am able to do this**?" "Yes, Lord," they replied. Then He touched their eyes and said, "**According to your faith will it be done to you**"; and their sight was restored...

Matthew 21:21-22
Jesus replied, "I tell you the truth, if you have faith and do not doubt, not only can you do what was done to the fig tree,

When You Pray for Healing - Believe You Received it and You Will Be Healed

but also you can say to this mountain *(sickness)*, 'Go throw yourself into the sea," and it will be done. **If you believe, you will receive whatever you ask for in prayer** (prayer for healing)."

Mark 9:23-25
"'If you can?" said Jesus. **"Everything is possible for him who believes."** Immediately the boy's father exclaimed, "I do believe; help me overcome my unbelief!" When Jesus saw the crowd was running to the scene, He rebuked the evil spirit. "You deaf and mute spirit," He said, "I command you come out of him and never enter him again."

Mark 11:23-24
"I tell you the truth, if anyone says to this mountain *(sickness)*, 'Go, throw yourself into the sea,' and does not doubt in his heart but believes that what he says will happen, it will be done for him. Therefore I tell you, whatever you ask for in prayer, **believe that you have received it, and it will be yours**."

Note by F.F. Bosworth: "Jesus authorizes us and commands us to put the blessing we pray for in past tense. He says, *when we ask* for what He offers, "Believe that it will be granted, and you will get it." We are to continue to believe that God gave us what we ask for when we prayed, and continue to praise and thank Him for what He has given us." - *Christ The Healer*

Luke 8:46-48
But Jesus said, "Someone touched Me; I know that power *(healing power)* has gone out from Me." ...In the presence of all the people, she told why she had touched Him and how

When You Pray for Healing - Believe You Received it and You Will Be Healed

she had been instantly healed. Then He said to her, "Daughter, **your faith has healed you**. Go in peace."

Author's Note: We also need to "touch" Jesus (through prayer and faith) to receive His healing power.

Luke 18:42
Jesus said to him, "Receive your sight; **your faith has healed you**."

John 11:40
Then Jesus said, "Did I not tell you that **if you believed, you would see the glory of God**?"

Acts 3:16
By faith in the Name of Jesus, this man whom you see and know was made strong. **It is Jesus' Name and the faith that comes through Him that has given this complete healing to him**, as you can all see.

Acts 14:8-10
In Lystra there sat a man crippled in his feet, who was lame from birth and had never walked. He listened to Paul as he was speaking. Paul looked directly at him, saw that **he had faith to be healed** and called out, "Stand up on your feet!" At that, **the man jumped up and began to walk**.

Author's Note: The crippled man's "faith to be healed" came when he heard and believed the message that Jesus Christ healed him. "Faith comes from hearing the message, and the message is heard through the word of Christ." – Romans 10:17

When You Pray for Healing - Believe You Received it and You Will Be Healed

Romans 1:16
I am not ashamed of the gospel, because it is the power of God for **salvation *(health)* of everyone who believes...**

Author's Note: The English word "salvation" is translated from the Greek word "soteria" and it means: health and eternal salvation.

Romans 4:19-21
Without weakening in his faith, he *(Abraham)* faced the fact that his body was as good as dead -since he was about a hundred years old -and Sarah's womb was also dead. Yet he did not waiver through unbelief regarding the Promises of God, but was strengthened in his faith and gave glory to God, **being fully persuaded that God had power to do that what he had promised *(healing)*.**

1 Corinthians 1:21
For since in the wisdom of God the world through its wisdom did not know Him, God was pleased through the foolishness of what was preached **to save *(heal)* those who believe**.

Author's Note: The English word "saved" is translated from the Greek word "sozo" and it means: heal and eternal salvation.

2 Corinthians 4:18
So we fix our eyes (the eyes of faith, your faith focus) not on what is seen *(not on our symptoms, circumstances, or sickness)*, but on what is unseen *(at God, at His promises, your complete healing, God's faithfulness and His justice)*. For what is seen is temporary *(subject to change)*, but what is unseen is eternal. (Notes by F.F. Bosworth)

Galatians 3:5
Does God give you His Spirit and work miracles among you because you observe the Law or because you believe what you have heard?

When You Pray for Healing - Believe You Received it and You Will Be Healed

Galatians 3:22
The Scripture declares that the whole world is a prisoner of sin, **so that what was promised** *(healing)*, **being given through faith in Jesus Christ, might be given to those who believe**.

Ephesians 1:19
and His incomparable great power *(healing power)* **for us who believe**. That power is like the working of His mighty strength,

Ephesians 2:8-9
For it is by grace you have been saved *(healed)*, **through faith** -- and this not from yourselves, **it is the gift of God**-- not by works, so that no one can boast.

Author's Note: Healing is a gift for everyone. The English word "saved" is translated from the Greek word "sozo" and it means: healed, made well, delivered from danger and eternal salvation.

Ephesians 3:12
In Him *(Jesus)* and **through faith in Him we may approach God with freedom and confidence** *(confidence to be healed)*.

Ephesians 6:16
In addition to all this, **take up the shield of faith,** with which you can extinguish all the flaming arrows *(sickness and disease)* of the evil one.

1 Thessalonians 2:13
when you received the Word *(healing promise)* of God, which you heard from us, you accepted it not as the word of

When You Pray for Healing - Believe You Received it and You Will Be Healed

men, but as it actually is, **the Word of God, which is at work** *(healing)* **in you who believe**.

Note by Harriet S. Bainbridge: "God's Word never fails to work in those that accept it as such, because they are not entertaining doubts as to its being fulfilled in their own experiences . . . God has given all blessing to Faith, He has none left to bestow upon unbelief."

Hebrews 4:16
Let us then approach the throne of grace with confidence *(confidence to be healed)*, so that we may receive mercy and find grace to help us in our time of need *(sickness)*.

Hebrews 11:6
And without faith *(faith to be healed)* it is impossible to please God, because anyone who comes to Him *(comes to Him for Healing)* **must believe** that He exists and that He rewards *(heals)* those who earnestly seek Him.

Hebrews 11:11
By faith Abraham, even though he was past age - and Sarah herself was barren - **was enabled to become a father because he considered Him faithful who made the promise**.

Author's Note: "Was enabled to become a father (receive the promise) because he considered Him faithful who made the promise."

Hebrews 11:32-35
David, Samuel and the prophets, who **through faith** conquered kingdoms, administered justice, and **gained what was promised** *(healing)*; who shut the mouths of lions,

When You Pray for Healing - Believe You Received it and You Will Be Healed

quenched the fury of the flames, and escaped the edge of the sword; whose weakness was turned to strength; and who became powerful in battle and routed foreign armies. Women received back their dead, raised to life again …

James 5:14-15
Is anyone of you sick? He should call the elders of the church to pray over him and anoint him with oil in the Name of the Lord. And **the prayer offered in faith will make the sick person well**; the Lord will raise him up. If he has sinned, he will be forgiven.

Author's Note: Anointing with oil is a symbol and sign of consecration.

1 John 5:14-15
This is the confidence we have in approaching God: that if we ask anything according to His will *(healing)*, He hears us. And if we know that He hears us—whatever we ask—we know that we have what we asked of Him.

Note by S.J. Hill: "In order for us to experience healing, we must be convinced from the Word that it's God's will for us to be healed. We must be so convinced that healing is a part of the Gospel and the redemption of Christ, that even the best arguments of men opposing this truth will be unable to sway us. When we know for certain it's God's will for us to be healed, it won't be difficult to believe He will do what we're sure He wants to do." - *God's Covenant of Healing*

"Let us put our sickness away by faith, as we would put away sin. The consecrated Christian will not consciously tolerate sin for a moment, and yet how tolerant some are towards sickness. They even pet and indulged their aches and pains, instead of resisting them as the words of the devil." – *Unknown author*

28
Persevere in Prayer and Faith for Healing

The Lord's promise is that "they will get well" (Mark 16:18), He does not say "instantly." - F.F. Bosworth

"How much effort are you willing to make in seeking Him? I hear people say they prayed and nothing happened. But often times it's a feeble attempt. Some are looking for instant results and when that doesn't happen, they quit. Instant results may not happen, but I encourage you to be diligent in your pursuit of the living God and become intimate with Him." – *Open my eyes Lord'* by Gary Oats

"God is not moved by repetition (Matthew 6:7); He is moved by faith. When we claim healing from the Lord and have to wait for its manifestation, we're to demonstrate persistence by reminding God of His promise. God loves to see His children believing His Word so strongly that we are willing to stand on it in spite of contrary circumstances. It was persistence that moved the heart of the unjust judge (Luke 18:1-8). How much more will persistent faith move the heart of our loving Father!"
– *God's Covenant of Healing* by S.J. Hill

Genesis 32:24, 26, 29
Jacob wrestled with the Man *(God)*. Then the Man *(God)* said, "Let Me go, for it is daybreak." But Jacob replied, "I will not let go you unless you bless *(heal)* me." ...Then He blessed him there.

Author's Note: Be like Jacob. Don't let go of God, the healing promise, and your faith to be healed until God heals you.

Isaiah 62:6-7
I have posted watchmen *(prayer warriors)* on your walls, O Jerusalem; they will never be silent day or night. You who

Persevere In Prayer and Faith for Healing

call on the LORD, give yourselves no rest, and give Him no rest till He establishes *(healing)* Jerusalem and makes her the praise of the earth.

Author's Note: You (prayer warriors) who call on the Lord give yourselves no rest (persistent faith-filled prayer), and give Him no rest until He establishes His healing promise in your life.

Matthew 5:41
It someone forces you to go one mile, go with him two miles.

Authors Note: Don't stop at one mile. Don't give up praying when you are just half way. The Lord wants you to go the distance (in prayer and faith) and receive your promise of healing.

Matthew 7:7-8 (AMP)
Keep on asking and it will be given you; **keep on seeking** and you will find; **keep on knocking** [reverently] and [the door] will be opened. For everyone who keeps on asking receives; and he who keeps on seeking finds; and to him who keeps knocking, [the door] will be opened.

Matthew 7:11 (AMP)
If you then, evil as you are, know how to give good *and* advantageous gifts to your children, how much more will your Father who is in heaven [perfect as He is] give good *and* advantageous things *(healing and restoration)* to those who **keep on asking Him**!

Luke 8:15
But the seed on good soil stands for those with a noble and good heart, who hear the Word *(healing promise)*, retain it, and **by persevering produce a crop**.

Luke 18:1
Then Jesus told His disciples a parable to show them that they should **always pray and not give up**.

Persevere In Prayer and Faith for Healing

Luke 18:7-8
"And **will not God bring about justice for His chosen ones, who cry out to Him day and night?** Will He keep putting them off? I tell you, He will see that they get justice, and quickly. However, when the Son of Man comes, will He find faith on earth?"

1 Corinthians 9:24
Do you not know that in a race all the runners run, but only one gets the prize? **Run *(persevere in prayer)* in such a way as to get the prize *(healing)*.**

Galatians 6:9
Let us not become weary in doing good *(persevering in prayer)*, for at the proper time we will reap a harvest **if we do not give up**.

1 Thessalonians 5:17-18
Pray continually; give thanks in all circumstances, for this is God's will for you in Christ Jesus.

Hebrew 3:14
We have come to share in Christ *(share in the healing Christ's provides)* if we hold firmly till the end the confidence (confidence for healing) we had at first *(when we first prayed for healing)*.

Hebrews 6:12
We do not want you to become lazy, but to imitate those who through faith and **patience *(persevering in prayer)* inherit what has been promised *(healing)*.**

Hebrews 6:15
And so after **waiting** *(persevering in prayer and faith)* **patiently**, Abraham received what was promised.

Persevere In Prayer and Faith for Healing

Hebrews 10:35-36
So do not throw away your confidence *(faith to be healed)*; it will be richly rewarded. **You need to persevere** so that when you have done the will of God, you will receive what *(healing promise)* He has promised.

James 5:11
As you know, we consider **blessed those who have persevered**. You have heard of Job's perseverance and have seen what the Lord **finally brought about**. The Lord is full of compassion and mercy.

Note by S.J. Hill: "There can be delays in the manifestation of the answer to our prayer because Satan will try to contest everything we embrace by faith. During wartime, whenever soldiers make an advance against their enemies, they usually end up having to "dig-in" under enemy fire. When we, as Christians, strive to advance in faith, we're also challenging our enemy. If we aren't prepared for the battle, Satan will keep us from coming into what rightfully belongs to us." – *God's Covenant of Healing*

1 Peter 5:8-10
Be self-controlled and alert. Your enemy the devil prowls around like a roaring lion looking for someone to devour. **Resist him, standing firm in the faith**, because you know that your brothers throughout the world are undergoing the same kind of sufferings. And the God of all grace, who called you to His eternal glory in Christ, after you have suffered a little while, will Himself restore you and make you strong, firm and steadfast.

Part 3
Scripture Principles For Healing

"You will know the truth, and the truth will set you free" (John 8:32). It is the truth of the written Word that sets us free – the truth known, understood, received, acted upon, maintained and steadfastly believed with an appropriating faith."
- *Christ The Healer* by F.F. Bosworth

29
Get Healed through Holy Living

Deuteronomy 23:14
For the LORD your God moves about in your camp to protect you and to deliver your enemies to you. Your camp must be holy, so that He will not see among you anything indecent and turn away from you.

2 Chronicles 7:14
If My people, who are called by My Name, will humble themselves and pray and seek My face and turn from their wicked ways, then will I hear from heaven and will forgive their sin and **will heal their land**.

2 Chronicles 16:30
For the eyes of the LORD range throughout the earth to strengthen those whose hearts are fully committed to Him.

Job 1:8-10
Then the LORD said to Satan, "Have you considered My servant Job? There is no one on earth like him; he is blameless and upright, a man who fears God and shuns evil." "Does Job fear God for nothing?" Satan replied. "Have you not put a hedge around him and his household and everything he has?"

Job 11:13-16
Yet if you devote your heart to Him and stretch out your hands to Him, if you put away the sin that is in your hand and allow no evil to dwell in your tent, then you will lift up your face without shame; you will stand firm and without fear. **You will surely forget your trouble *(sickness)*, recalling it only as waters gone by**.

Get Healed through Holy Living

Job 17:9
Nevertheless, the righteous will hold to their ways, and **those with clean hands** will grow stronger.

Psalm 32:6-7
Therefore let everyone who is godly pray to You while you may be found; surely when the mighty waters rise, they will not reach him. You are my hiding place; You will protect me from trouble and surround me with songs of deliverance.

Psalm 34:9
Fear the Lord you His saints, **those who fear Him lack nothing**.

Psalm 34:15
The eyes of the Lord are on the righteous and His ears attentive to their cry

Psalm 37:28
For the Lord loves the just and will not forsake His faithful ones. **They will be protected forever**, but the offspring of the wicked will be cut off;

Psalm 84:11
For the LORD God is a sun and shield; the LORD bestows favor and honor; **no good thing *(healing)* does He withhold from those whose walk is blameless**.

Psalm 128:1-2
Blessed are all who fear the LORD, who walk in His ways. You will eat the fruit of your labor; blessings and prosperity will be yours.

Proverbs 3:7-8
Do not be wise in your own eyes; fear the LORD and shun

Get Healed through Holy Living

evil. This will bring health to your body and nourishment to your bones.

Proverbs 3:34
He mocks proud mockers **but gives grace** *(healing grace)* **to the humble.**

Jeremiah 32:19
great are Your purposes and mighty are Your deeds. Your eyes are open to all the ways of men; You reward *(and heal)* everyone according to his conduct and as his deeds deserve.

Micah 2:7
…"Do not My Words *(healing promises)* do good **to him whose ways are upright?**"

Matthew 6:33
But seek first His kingdom and His righteousness, and all these things *(healing)* will be given to you as well.

Matthew 5:8
Blessed are the pure in heart, for they will see God.

Author's Note: "Blessed are the pure in heart, for they will see God" move in their life.

John 15:7-8
If you remain in Me and My Words remain in you, ask whatever you wish *(healing)*, and it will be given you. This is to My Father's glory, that you my bear much fruit, showing yourselves to be My disciples.

Get Healed through Holy Living

John 15:16
"You did not choose Me, but I chose you and appointed you to **go and bear fruit—fruit *(holy living)* that will last. Then** the Father will give you whatever you ask (healing) in My Name."

2 Corinthians 7:1
Since we have these promises *(healing promises)*, dear friends let us purify ourselves from everything that contaminates body and spirit, perfecting holiness out of reverence for God.

1 Timothy 2:15
But women will be saved *(sozo)* through childbearing--if they continue in faith, love and holiness with propriety.

Author's Note: The English word "saved" is translated from the Greek word "sozo" and it means: healed and eternal salvation.

Hebrews 5:7
During the days of Jesus' life on earth, He offered up prayers and petitions with loud cries and tears to the One who could save Him from death, and **He was heard because of His reverent submission**.

James 1:21
Therefore, **get rid of all moral filth and the evil that is so prevalent and humbly accept the Word planted in you**, which can save *(heal)* you.

Author's Note: The English word "save" is translated from the Greek word "sozo" and it means: healed and eternal salvation.

Get Healed through Holy Living

James 4:8b-10 (NLT)
Clean up your hearts, you who want to follow the sinful ways of the world and God at the same time. Be sorry for your sins and cry because of them. Be sad and do not laugh. Let your joy be turned to sorrow. Let yourself be brought low before the Lord. **Then He will lift you up and help** *(heal)* **you**.

James 5:16
Therefore **confess your sins to each other and pray for each other so that you may be healed**. The prayer of a righteous man is powerful and effective.

1 Peter 3:12a
For the eyes of the Lord are on the righteous and His ears are attentive to their prayer *(healing prayer)*,

1 Peter 5:5-6
…All of you, **clothe yourselves with humility toward one another**, because, "God opposes the proud but **gives grace** *(healing grace)* **to the humble**." Humble yourselves, therefore, under God's mighty hand, that He may lift you up *(lift you up out of sickness)* in due time.

1 John 3:21-22
Dear friends, if our hearts do not condemn us, we have confidence before God and receive from Him anything we ask *(healing)*, **because we obey His commands and do what pleases Him**.

30
Get Healed Through Giving

Psalm 112:5
Good *(healing)* will come to him who is **generous and lends freely**, who conducts his affairs with justice.

Proverbs 19:17
He who is kind to the poor lends to the LORD, and He will reward *(healing)* him for what he has done.

Proverbs 22:9
A generous man will himself be blessed *(healed)*, for he shares his food with the poor.

Proverbs 28:27
He who gives to the poor will lack nothing, but he who closes his eyes to them receives many curses.

Isaiah 58:6-8
"Is not this the kind of fasting I have chosen: to loose the chains of injustice and untie the cords of the yoke, to set the oppressed free and break every yoke? Is it not to **share your food with the hungry and to provide the poor wanderer with shelter - when you see the naked, to clothe him, and not to turn away from your own flesh and blood? Then** your light will break forth like the dawn, and your healing will quickly appear; then your righteousness will go before you, the glory of the Lord will be your rear guard. Then you will call, and the Lord will answer; you will cry for help, and He will say: Here I am.

Malachi 3:10-11 (AMP)
Bring all the tithes *(a tenth of your income)* into the storehouse, that there may be food in My house, and prove Me now by it, says the Lord of Hosts, if I will not open the

Get Healed Through Giving

windows of heaven for you and pour a blessing, that there shall not be room enough to receive it. **And I will rebuke the devourer** [insects and plagues] *(sickness)* for your sakes...

Author's Note: When you bring in the whole tithe, God will rebuke the devourer (Satan), from afflicting you.

Matthew 5:7
"Blessed are the merciful, for they will be shown mercy *(healing mercy)*."

Matthew 6:3-4
But when you give to the needy, do not let your left hand know what your right hand is doing, so that your giving may be in secret. Then your Father, who sees what is done in secret, will reward you.

1 Peter 3:9
Do not repay evil with evil or insult with insult, **but with blessing, because to this you were called so that you may inherit a blessing** *(healing)*.

31
Get Healed Through Praise, Worship and Thanksgiving

"Since it is "by His wounds you have been healed," let us not forget what healing cost, but with gratitude and love, and consecrated service to God, let us stand on His promise and "blow the rams horn" of faith and thanksgiving and praise until the wall of our affliction fall down flat." – *Christ The Healer* by F.F. Bosworth

Exodus 23:25
Worship the Lord your God, and His blessing will be on your food and water. I will take away sickness from among you,

Psalm 31:19 (AMP)
Oh, how great is Your goodness *(good health)*, which You have laid up for those who fear, revere, *and* worship You, goodness *(healing)* which You have wrought for those who trust and take refuge in You before the sons of men!

Psalm 33:18-19 (AMP)
Behold, the Lord's eyes are upon those who fear [who revere and worship Him with awe], who wait for Him and hope in His mercy and loving-kindness, **to deliver them** from death and keep them alive in famine.

Psalm 50:14-15
Sacrifice thank offerings *(praise)* to God, fulfill your vows to the Most High, and call upon Me in the day of trouble; I will deliver you, and you will honor Me.

Psalm 68:19
Praise be to the Lord, to God our Savior, who daily bears our burdens.

Get Healed Through Praise, Worship and Thanksgiving

Psalm 103:1-3
Praise the Lord, O my soul; all my inmost being, praise His holy Name. Praise the LORD, O my soul, and forget not all His benefits - who forgives all your sins and heals all your diseases,

Psalm 139:14
I will praise You because I am fearfully and wonderfully made; Your works are wonderful I know that full well.

Proverbs 3:7-8 (AMP)
Be not wise in your own eyes; reverently fear and worship the Lord and turn [entirely] away from evil. It shall be health to your nerves and sinews, and marrow and moistening to your bones.

Isaiah 49:13 (NKJ)
Sing (praise), O heavens! Be joyful, O earth! And break out in singing (worshiping), O mountains! For the LORD has comforted His people, and will have mercy on His afflicted.

Jeremiah 17:14
Heal me, O LORD, and I will be healed; save me and I will be saved, for You are the One I praise.

Jonah 2:8-10 (KJV)
They that observe lying vanities *(symptoms)* forsake their own mercy. But I will sacrifice unto thee; with a voice of thanksgiving *(praise)*; ... And the Lord spake unto the fish, and it vomited out Jonah upon the dry land.

Note by F.F. Bosworth: "Jonah in full-faith, when in the middle of a seemly impossible situation inside the fish acted out his faith in God for deliverance by praising and thanking God in advance. This is God's appointed way for our appropriation of all His blessings."

Get Healed Through Praise, Worship and Thanksgiving

Malachi 4:2 (AMP)
But unto you who revere and worshipfully fear My name shall the Sun of Righteousness arise with healing in His wings and His beams, and you shall go forth and gambol like calves [released] from the stall and leap for joy.

Matthew 8:1-3 (NKJ)
When He had come down from the mountain, great crowds followed Him. And behold, **a leper came and worshipped Him** saying, "Lord, if You are willing, You can make me clean." The Jesus put out His hand and touched him, saying, "I am willing; be cleansed." And immediately his leprosy was cleansed.

32
Get Healed and Delivered from Demonic Affliction Through Praise and Worship

Exodus 17:11, 13, 15-16
As long as Moses held up his hands, the Israelites were winning ... So Joshua overcame the Amalekite army with the sword ... Moses built an alter and called it The Lord is my Banner *("Victor")*. He said, "**For hands were lifted up** *(worship and praise)* to throne of the Lord. The Lord will be at war against the Amalekites *(demonic forces)* from generation to generation."

Author's Note: "I will praise You as long as I live, and in Your Name **I will lift up my hands**." - Psalm 63:4

1 Samuel 16:23 (AMP)
And when the evil spirit from God was upon Saul, David took a lyre and played it (praise and worship); so Saul was refreshed and became well, and the evil spirit left him.

2 Kings 17:39
Rather, worship the Lord your God; it is He who will deliver you from the hand of all your enemies *(demonic sickness and oppression)*.

2 Chronicles 20:18, 22
Jehoshaphat bowed with his face to the ground, and all the people of Judah and Jerusalem fell down in worship before the Lord. As they began to sing and praise, the Lord set ambushes against the men *(or demons of affliction)* of Ammon and Moab and Mount Seir who were invading Judah, and they were defeated.

Author's Note: Our battle is not against men, but against demons and demonic affliction (Ephesians 6:12). But the principle of worshiping God in spiritual warfare still stands and it will cause our enemy (Satan and his demons) to be defeated.

Get Healed and Delivered from Demonic Affliction Through Praise and Worship

Psalm 24:7-8
Lift up your heads, O you gates *(praise)*; be lifted up, you ancient doors *(praise)*, that the King of Glory may come in. Who is the King of Glory? The Lord strong and mighty, the Lord mighty in battle.

Author's Note: Isaiah 60:18 says, "your gates are praise."
So lift up your heads to worship and praise Him that the King of Glory, the Lord mighty in battle, may come in to heal and deliver you from demonic oppression.

Psalm 34:7 (AMP)
The Angel of the Lord encamps around those who fear Him [who revere and worship Him with awe] and each of them He delivers.

Psalm 35:27
May those who delight in My vindication shout for joy and gladness; **may they always say, "The LORD be exalted**, who delights in the well-being *(good health)* of His servant."

Isaiah 30:32
Every stroke the Lord lays on them *(demons of affliction and oppression)* with His punishing rod will be to the music of tambourines and harps *(worship and praise)*, as He fights them *(demons)* in battle with the blows of His arm.

Acts 16:25-26
About midnight Paul and Silas were praying and singing hymns to God, and the other prisoners were listening to them. Suddenly there was such a violent earthquake that the foundations of the prison were shaken. At once all the prison doors flew open, and everybody's chains *(chains of oppression)* came loose.

Note by F.F. Bosworth: "Paul and Silas sang praises at midnight with their backs bleeding and their feet in shackles, and God sang bass with an earthquake, which set them free."

33
Get Healed Through Godly, Healthy and Positive Thoughts

Author's Note: These Scripture truths may be the most important principles to understand and endeavor to live out, in order to live the healthy faith-filled life God has provided. These powerful principles that relate to our thought life are guaranteed by God to affect the outcome of a person's life – for good and bad in everyway.

Satan knows these principles are true which is why he attacks our minds more than any other area in our life. He knows that if he can apply strongholds to our minds he will affect the course and health of our life. Satan applies strongholds of doubt and unbelief, un-forgiveness, fear, ungodly thoughts, false symptoms, and lies of all kinds.

We need to ask the Holy Spirit in prayer to tell us what strongholds (thoughts or lies) we believe. So that we can repent of them, renounce them and command them off our life in Jesus Name. "We have divine power to demolish strongholds and we take captive of every thought to make it obedient to Christ." (2 Corinthians 10:4-5)

"Whenever we are affected by any other voice more than the voice of God, we have forsaken the Lord's way for our healing."
- *Christ The Healer* by F.F. Bosworth

"If a person feeds on negative thoughts throughout the day, every task or every trial that comes his way will be approached from a defeated attitude before he even under takes it. However, we have the ability, through the Word of God, to *speak* God's Word throughout the day and rewire our negative thoughts, which will then bring healing and health to the body and mind."
- *The Bible Cure For Depression and Anxiety* by Don Colbert, M.D.

Get Healed Through Godly, Healthy and Positive Thoughts

Proverbs 4:23 (NLT)
Guard your heart *(mind, feelings and imagination)* above all else, for it determines the course of your life (healing).

Author's Note: The English word "heart" here is translated from the Hebrew word "Leb" and it means: mind, feelings and imagination.

Proverbs 4:23 (CEV)
Carefully guard your thoughts because they are the source of true life.

Proverbs 14:30a (NLT)
A peaceful heart *(mind)* leads to a healthy body;

Proverbs 15:15b (AMP)
he who has a glad heart has a continual feast [regardless of the circumstances].

Proverbs 17:22a
A cheerful heart *(mind)* is good medicine

Proverbs 23:7a (NKJ)
For as he *(a person)* **thinks in his heart, so is he**.

Matthew 12:33
"**Make a tree *(your thoughts)* good and its fruit *(life)* will be good *(healed)***, or make a tree bad and its fruit will be bad, for a tree is recognized by its fruit."

Get Healed Through Godly, Healthy and Positive Thoughts

Matthew 23:26
"Blind Pharisees! First clean the inside of the cup and dish, and then the outside also will be clean."

Author's Note: Jesus is saying clean up your heart and thoughts and the results will be an outwardly clean, holy and healthy life.

Luke 6:45
"The good man brings *(produces)* good things *(healed and healthy life)* out of the good stored up in his heart *(thoughts and mind)*, and the evil man brings evil things out of the evil stored up in his heart."

Author's Note: The English word "heart" here is translated from the Greek word "kardia" and it means: thoughts and mind.

Romans 12:1-2 (AMP)
Do not be conformed to this world –this age, fashioned after and adapted to its external, superficial customs. But be transformed *(changed)* by the [entire] renewal of your mind – by its new ideals and its new attitude – **so that you may prove [for yourselves] what is the good and acceptable and perfect will of God, even the thing which is good and acceptable and perfect [in His sight for you].**

Note by F. F. Bosworth: "The mind and thoughts of those seeking healing must be "renewed" so as to be brought into harmony with the mind of God as revealed in the Bible. Faith for God's promised blessing is the result of knowing and acting on God's Word. The right mental attitude or the "renewed mind" makes steadfast faith possible at all. God always heals when He can get the right cooperation." - *Christ The Healer*

Philippians 4:8-9
Finally, brothers, whatever is true, whatever is noble, whatever is right, whatever is pure, whatever is lovely, whatever is admirable-- if anything is excellent or praiseworthy--**think about such things. …And the God of peace will be with you**.

Get Healed Through Godly, Healthy and Positive Thoughts

3 John 2
Dear friend, I pray that you may enjoy good health and **that all may go well with you, even as your soul is getting along well**.

Author's Note: The English word "soul" is translated from the Greek word "psyche" and it means: mind, heart and life.

34
Get Healed by Having a Godly, Healthy and Positive Confession

"If God's Word says we're healed, we would be foolish to confess otherwise. To confess healing even in the face of adverse circumstances is simply an act of obedience to God's admonition to believe He has heard and answered our prayer (Mark 11:23-24; 1 John 5:14-15). Speaking the Word of God, especially in time of difficulty, glorifies the Lord. What could please Him more than hearing His people boldly voicing their faith in their heavenly Father in the midst of seemingly adverse circumstances?"
- *God's Covenant of Healing* by S.J. Hill

"The confession of your lips that has grown out of faith in your heart will absolutely defeat the enemy in every combat. Christ's words broke the power of demons and healed the sick. They do the same today when we believe and confess them. The Word will heal you if you continually confess it. God will make your body obey your confession of His Word; "no word of God is void of power" (Luke 1:37 ASV). Before being conscious of any physical change, faith rejoices and says, "It is written," and believing what is written. Jesus won His great victories by saying, "It is written," and believing what was written."
– *Christ The Healer* by F.F. Bosworth

Psalm 35:27
May those who delight in My vindication shout for joy and gladness; **may they always say**, "The LORD be exalted, Who delights in the well-being *(good health)* of His servant."

Proverbs 10:11a
The mouth of the righteous is a fountain of life,

[Author's Note: When our confession agrees with the healing promises of God, it positions us to receive them and we will receive them.]

Get Healed by Having a Godly, Healthy and Positive Confession

Proverbs 10:21
The lips of the righteous nourish many but fools die for lack of judgment.

Proverbs 12:14
From the fruit of his lips a man is filled with good things *(healed and healthy life)* as surely as the work of his hands rewards him.

Proverbs 12:18b
the tongue of the wise brings healing.

Proverbs 13:2a
From the fruit of his lips a man enjoys good things *(healing)*,

Proverbs 13:3
He who guards his lips guards his life *(health)*, but he who speaks rashly comes to ruin.

Proverbs 15:4a
The tongue that brings healing is a tree of life,

Proverbs 16:24
Pleasant words are like a honey comb, sweet to the soul and healing to the bones.

Proverbs 18:20
From the fruit of his mouth a man's a stomach is filled; **with the harvest of his lips he is satisfied *(healed and healthy)***.

Proverbs 18:21 (AMP)
Death and life are in the power of the tongue and they who indulge in it shall eat the fruit *(healing)* of it [for death or life].

Get Healed by Having a Godly, Healthy and Positive Confession

Isaiah 44:24-26
"This is what the LORD says -- Your Redeemer, who formed you in the womb: I am the LORD, who has made all things, who alone stretched out the heavens, who spread out the earth by myself, **who carries out the words** *(healing words and prayers)* **of His servants** and fulfills the predictions of His messengers,

Joel 3:10b
Let the weakling say, "I am strong."

Matthew 21:21
Jesus replied, "I tell you the truth, if you have faith and do not doubt, not only can you do what was done to the fig tree, but also you can **say to this mountain** *(sickness)*, 'Go throw yourself into the sea," and it will be done.

Author's Note: Here faith and our confession are working together to accomplish God's purpose.

Romans 10:10
For it is with your heart that you believe and are justified, and it is **with your mouth you confess and are saved** *(healed)*.

Author's Note: The English word "saved" is translated from the Greek word "sozo" and it means: healed, cured, preserved, be made whole, made well, deliverance from suffering and eternal salvation.

2 Corinthians 4:13
It is written: "I believed; therefore I have spoken. With that same spirit of faith we also believe and therefore speak,

Note by S.J. Hill: "According to Christ, believing with the heart

Get Healed by Having a Godly, Healthy and Positive Confession

that the mountain will move is not enough. What's in the heart must be expressed with the mouth. It's what the Apostle Paul referenced to in 2 Corinthians 4:13." – *God's Covenant of Healing*

Hebrew 4:14 (ESV)
Since then we have a great High Priest who has passed through the heavens, Jesus, the Son of God, **let us hold fast our confession** *(The confession of our faith in the redemptive work that God provided in Christ).*

Author's Note: We are told to "hold fast" to the confession of the salvation of Christ in all its fullness. "Hold fast" that Calvary has freed you. "Hold fast" to the confession that "The Sovereign LORD is my strength." "Hold fast" to the confession that, "Surely He hath borne my sickness and carried my diseases," and that "By His wounds you have been healed." "Hold fast" to the confession that, "He has given you authority to trample on snakes and scorpions and to overcome all the power of the enemy and nothing will harm you."

James 3:4-5
Or take ships as an example. Although they are so large and are driven by strong winds, **they are steered by a very small rudder wherever the pilot wants to go. Likewise the tongue**…

Author's Note: "Likewise the tongue" is a small part of the body and it steers our life and sets the whole course of our life.

1 Peter 3:10
For, "Whoever would love life and **see good days** must keep his tongue from evil and his lips from deceitful speech.

Revelation 12:11
They overcame him *(satan)* by the blood of the lamb and **by the word of their testimony**.

Part 4
Reasons You Can Be Confident For Healing

This is the confidence we have in approaching God: that if we ask anything according to His will *(healing)*, He hears us. And if we know that He hears us—whatever we ask—we know that we have what we asked of Him.
- 1 John 5:14-15

35
God Has a Healing Contract with You

"If, after coming to God for healing, He finds you more encouraged by your improvement than by His Word, He may find it necessary to test your faith, in order to teach you the glorious lesson of believing His Word, when every sense contradicts Him. Faith has to do only with the Word of God. What God has promised *belongs* to us. We have a *right* to what He promises us."
- *Christ The Healer* by F.F. Bosworth

2 Samuel 7:28
O Sovereign Lord, You are God! Your words are trustworthy, and You have promised these good things *(healing promises)* to Your servant.

2 Samuel 22:31
"As for God, His way is perfect; **the Word *(healing word)* of the LORD is flawless.** He is a shield for all who take refuge in Him.

1 Kings 8:56
"Praise be to the LORD, Who has given rest to His people Israel just as He promised. **Not one Word has failed of all the good Promises *(healing promises)* He gave** through His servant Moses.

Nehemiah 9:8b
You *(Lord)* have kept Your promise because You are righteous.

Psalm 89:34
I will not violate My Covenant *(healing and protection covenant)* or alter what My lips have uttered.

God Has a Healing Contract with You

Psalm 107:20
He sent forth His Word and healed them; He rescued them from the grave.

Psalm 119:89
Your Word *(healing Word)*, **O Lord, is eternal; it stands firm in the heavens.**

Psalm 138:2
I will bow down toward Your holy temple and will praise Your name for Your love and Your faithfulness, **for You have exalted above all things Your Name and Your Word** *(healing Word)*.

Psalm 145:13
Your kingdom is an everlasting kingdom, and Your dominion endures through all generations. **The LORD is faithful to all His promises** *(healing promises)* and loving toward all He has made.

Isaiah 40:8
"The grass withers and the flowers fall, but **the Word** *(healing Word)* **of our God stands forever.**"

Isaiah 55:10-11
As the rain and the snow come down from heaven, and do not return to it without watering the earth and making it bud and flourish, so that it yields seed for the sower and bread for the eater, **so is My Word** *(healing promise)* **that goes out from My mouth: It will not return to Me empty, but will accomplish what I desire and achieve the purpose** *(healing)* **for which I sent it.**

Jeremiah 1:12
The LORD said to me, "You have seen correctly, for **I am**

God Has a Healing Contract with You

watching to see that My Word *(healing Scripture)* **is fulfilled."**

Matthew 4:4
Jesus answered, "It is written: 'Man does not live by bread alone, but on every Word *(healing promise)* that comes from the mouth of God.'"

Matthew 24:35
"Heaven and earth will pass away, but **My Words** *(healing promises)* **will never pass away."**

Mark 16:20
Then the disciples went out and preached everywhere, and the Lord worked with them and **confirmed His Word** *(healing promise)* **by the signs that accompanied it**.

2 Corinthians 1:20
For no matter how many Promises *(healing promises)* God has made, they are "Yes" in Christ. And so through Him the "Amen" is spoken by us to the glory of God.

Hebrews 4:12
For the Word *(healing word)* **of God is living and active**. Sharper than any double-edged sword, **it penetrates** ...

Note from Gems of Truth on Divine Healing: "As we claim the healing Word, in faith receiving the finished work of Jesus, the "sword of the Spirit" sticks a death blow to disease. Faith sees God in His Love and omnipotence making good the Word."

James 1:21
Therefore, get rid of all moral filth and the evil that is so prevalent and **humbly accept the Word** *(healing word)* **planted in you, which can save** *(heal)* **you**.

36
Jesus Loves to Answer Prayer for Healing

"Christ authorizes us to consider our prayer answered the moment we pray. Faith believes God has already done what we ask Him to do. We are to believe it is done, not because we see it done, but because God's Word declares it done. When God's Word is the only basis for believing our prayer is answered, we can have the assurance that our faith is strong. God will not begin to manifest our healing until after we believe He has heard our prayer (1 John 5:14-15). The manifestation always comes after we believe. It may come a moment after we pray; then again, it may come a week, a month, or even longer before the answer is visible. Yet, if we expect to see the answer, we must receive it by faith even before we see it manifested."
 - *God's Covenant of Healing* by S.J. Hill

"When coming to Jesus for healing, let's keep in mind that we are not asking Him to do something unusual for us. Instead, we must understand that He is more than willing to have us share in what He has already provided through His death and resurrection." – *God's Covenant of Healing* by S.J. Hill

1 Kings 3:5
God said, "Ask for whatever *(healing)* you want me to give you."

Author's Note: But whatever you ask in prayer, you must believe you have received it, the moment you pray for it. - Mark 11:24

Psalm 3:4
To the LORD I cry aloud, and **He answers *(heals)* me** from His holy hill.

Jesus Loves to Answer Prayer for Healing

Psalm 5:3
In the morning, O LORD, You hear my voice; in the morning **I lay my requests** *(to be healed and healthy)* **before You and wait in expectation.**

Psalm 9:10
Those who know Your Name will trust in You, for **You, Lord, have never forsaken those who seek You**.

Psalm 9:12b
He does not ignore the cry of the afflicted.

Psalm 21:1-2
O LORD, the king rejoices in Your strength. How great is his joy in the victories You give! **You have granted him the desire of his heart** *(to be healed)* **and have not withheld the request** *(request for healing)* **of his lips**.

Psalm 37:4
Delight yourself in the LORD and He will give you the desires *(healing)* of your heart.

Psalm 86:7
In the day of my trouble I will call to You, for **You will answer** *(heal)* **me**.

Psalm 91:15
He will call upon Me, and I will answer *(restore and heal)* **him**; I will be with him in trouble, I will deliver him and honor him.

Psalm 102:17
He will respond to the prayer of the destitute; He will not despise their plea.

Jesus Loves to Answer Prayer for Healing

Psalm 138:3
When I called *("heal me Lord")*, You answered me; You made me bold and stouthearted.

Psalm 145:16
You open Your hand and satisfy the desires of every living thing.

Proverbs 10:24b
what the righteous desire *(healing)* will be granted.

Proverbs 11:23a
The desire of the righteous ends only in good *(healing and health)*,

Isaiah 19:22b
They will turn to the Lord, and **He will respond to their pleas and heal them**.

Isaiah 30:19
O people of Zion, who live in Jerusalem, you will weep no more. How gracious He will be when you cry for help! **As soon as He hears, He will answer *(heal)* you**.

Isaiah 65:24
Before they call I will answer; while they are still speaking I will hear.

Jonah 2:1-2
From inside the fish Jonah prayed to the LORD his God. He said: "**In my distress I called to the LORD, and He answered *(healed and delivered)* me**. From the depths of the grave I called for help, and You listened to my cry."

Jesus Loves to Answer Prayer for Healing

Zechariah 13:9
This third I will bring into the fire; I will refine them like silver and test them like gold. **They will call on My Name and I will answer *(heal)* them**; I will say, 'They are My people,' and they will say, 'The Lord is our God.'

Matthew 6:6
"But when you pray, go into your room, close the door and pray to your Father, who is unseen. **Then your Father, who sees what is done in secret, will reward you.**"

Matthew 6:10
Your kingdom come, Your will be done on earth as it is in heaven.

Note by S.J. Hill: "Since there's no sickness in heaven, it must be the Father's will and desire that there be no sickness among His people on earth." - *God's Covenant of Healing*

Matthew 7:7
"**Ask *(for healing)* and it will be given to you**; seek and you will find; knock and the door will be opened to you.

Matthew 7:9-11
"Which of you, if his son asks for bread, will give him a stone? Or if he asks for a fish, will give him a snake? If you, then, though you are evil, know how to give good gifts to your children, **how much more will your Father in heaven give good gifts *(healing and restoration)* to those who ask Him!**"

Matthew 18:19
"Again, I tell you that **if two of you on earth agree about anything *(healing)* you ask for, it will be done for you by My Father in heaven.**"

Jesus Loves to Answer Prayer for Healing

John 14:13-14
"And **I will do whatever you ask in My Name**, so that the Son may bring glory to the Father. You may **ask Me for anything** *(healing)* **in My Name, and I will do it**."

John 16:23-24
In that day you will no longer ask Me anything. **I tell you the truth, My Father will give** *(heal)* **you whatever you ask in My Name**. Until now you have not asked for anything in My Name. **Ask and you will receive** *(be healed)***, and your joy will be complete**."

Acts 3:26
When God raised up His Servant, He sent Him first to you to bless you

Romans 10:12
For there is no difference between Jew and Gentile—the same Lord is Lord of all and **richly blesses** *(heals and delivers)* **all who call on Him**.

Ephesians 3:20
Now to Him who is able to do immeasurably **more than all we ask or imagine**, according to His power *(healing power)* at work within us ...

37
Your Redemption from Sickness was Prophesied

Introduction by Author:

Spiritual healing, emotional healing, relational healing, physical healing, and long life are inseparable elements in the redemption Jesus Christ paid for at Calvary.

There are two significant words in Old Testament messianic prophecies recorded in the book of Isaiah the prophet and the Psalms. These words reveal God's redemptive will for healing the whole person through the sacrifice of Jesus Christ at Calvary. These Hebrew words are *choli* and *mak'ob*. *Choli* is interpreted as <u>disease and sickness</u> and *mak'ob* is interpreted as <u>pains, suffering and woes</u>.

At the beginning of His earthly ministry Jesus testified to these Old Testament prophesies when He proclaimed Himself to be the One who provides healing redemption (Luke 4:17-19). The Holy Spirit also testifies and confirms these prophesies elsewhere in the New Testament (Matthew 8:17, 1 Peter 2:24).
Praise and thank the Lord with a grateful heart in full confidence and receive His free gift of healing redemption. Your healing is paid for (redeemed) in full.

<u>Isaiah 53</u> (*Young's Literal Translation* by Dr. Young)

Vs 3: He *(Jesus)* is despised, and left of men, A man of pains *(Hebrew: mak'ob)*, and acquainted with sickness *(choli)*, And as One hiding the face from us, He is despised, and we esteemed Him not.

Vs 4: Surely our sicknesses *(choli)* He hath borne, And our pains *(mak'ob)* -- He hath carried them, And we -- we have esteemed Him plagued, Smitten of God, and afflicted.

Your Redemption from Sickness was Prophesied

Vs 5: And He is pierced for our transgressions, Bruised for our iniquities, The chastisement of our peace [is] on Him, And by His bruise there is healing to us.

Vs 6: All of us like sheep have wandered, Each to his own way we have turned, And Jehovah hath caused to meet on Him, The punishment of us all.

Vs 10: And Jehovah hath delighted to bruise Him, He hath made Him sick *(choli)*, If His soul doth make an offering for guilt, He seeth seed -- He prolongeth days, And the pleasure of Jehovah in His hand doth prosper.

Vs 12: Therefore I give a portion to Him among the many, And with the mighty He apportioneth spoil, Because that He exposed to death His soul, And with transgressors He was numbered, And He the sin of many hath borne, And for transgressors He intercedeth.

Isaiah 53:3-5, 10 (Dr. Isaac Leeser, Translator of *The Hebrew - English Bible*)
3 He was despised and shunned of men; A man of pains and acquainted with disease. 4 But only our diseases did He bear himself, and our pains He carried. 5 And through His bruises was healing granted to us. ... 10 But the Lord was pleased to crush Him through disease.

Isaiah 50:6
I offered My back to those who **beat** Me, My cheeks to those who pulled out My beard; I did not hide My face from mocking and spitting. *("Beat" for your physical redemption)*

Author's Note: "With His stripes (put on His "back" by "those who beat Him") we are healed." – Isaiah 53:5 KJV, *(physical redemption)*

Your Redemption from Sickness was Prophesied

Isaiah 52:14
Just as there were many who were appalled at Him —His appearance was so **disfigured** beyond that of any man and His form **marred** beyond human likeness— *(disfigured and marred for your physical redemption)*

Isaiah 53:4-5
Surely He *(Jesus)* took up our infirmities and carried our sorrows *(pains and suffering)*, yet we considered Him stricken by God, smitten by Him, and afflicted. But He was **pierced for our transgressions'** He was **crushed for our iniquities** *(for our spiritual redemption)*; **the punishment that brought us peace** *(for our mental, emotion and relational redemption)* **was upon Him**, and **by His wounds we are healed** *(we have physical redemption)*.

Author's Note: "Sorrows" - the Hebrew word used here is "mak'ob" and when translated means: pain, suffering and woes.

Isaiah 53:11a
After the **suffering of His soul**, He will see the light of life and be satisfied; *(Suffered for your mental and emotional redemption)*

Psalm 103:2-3
Praise the Lord, O my soul, and forget not all His benefits - Who forgives all your sins and heals all your diseases,

Psalm 107:20
The Lord sent forth His Word *(Jesus)* and healed them *(physical healing)*; He rescued them from the grave *(spiritual healing)*.

Author's Note: "The Word *(Jesus)* became flesh and made His dwelling among us." - John 1:14

Psalm 130:7
O Israel put your hope in the LORD, for with the LORD is unfailing love and with Him is **full** *(spiritual, physical and emotional)* redemption.

Your Redemption from Sickness was Prophesied

Matthew 8:17
This was to fulfill what was spoken through the Prophet Isaiah: "He *(Jesus)* took up *(at Calvary)* our infirmities and carried our diseases."

Matthew 27:47
Jesus cried out in a loud voice ... "My God, My God, why have You **forsaken** Me?" *(Forsaken for your spiritual and emotional rejection, and abandonment redemption.)*

Luke 4:17-19 (AMP)
"And there was handed to Him [the roll of] the book of the prophet Isaiah. He opened (unrolled) the book and found the place where it was written, [Isaiah 61:1, 2.] The Spirit of the Lord [is] upon Me, because He has anointed Me [the Anointed One, the Messiah] to preach the good news (the Gospel) to the poor; He has sent Me to announce release to the captives and recovery of sight to the blind, to send forth as delivered those who are oppressed [who are downtrodden, bruised, crushed, and broken down by calamity], To proclaim the acceptable year of the Lord [the day when salvation and the free favors of God profusely abound. [Isaiah 61:1, 2.]

John 12:38-41 (NLT)
This is exactly what the prophet Isaiah predicted: "LORD, who has believed Our Message? To whom has the LORD revealed His powerful arm?" But the people couldn't believe, for Isaiah also said ... their hearts cannot understand, and they cannot turn to Me *(Jesus)* and have Me heal them." Isaiah was referring to Jesus when he said this, because he saw the future and spoke of the Messiah's glory.

Acts 13:47 – Isaiah 49:6
For this is what the Lord has commanded us: "'I have made

Your Redemption from Sickness was Prophesied

You *(Jesus)* a light for the Gentiles, that you may bring salvation *(health)* to the ends of the earth.'"

Author's Note: The English word "salvation" is translated from the Greek word "soteria" and it means: health and eternal salvation.

2 Corinthians 5:21
God made Him *(Jesus)* who had no sin *(of His own)* to be sin for us, so that in Him we might become the righteousness of the God.

Author's Note: Likewise, God made Him who had no sickness to be sickness for us ("Surely our sicknesses He hath borne, and our pains -- He hath carried them, and we -- we have esteemed Him plagued, Smitten of God, and afflicted – Isaiah 53:4 YLT), so that in Him we might become the healed of the Lord.

Hebrews 9:28a
so Christ was sacrificed once to take away the sins of many people;

Author's Note: Likewise, He was sacrificed once to take away sickness of many people.

Hebrews 10:5 (NLV)
When Christ came into the world, He said to God, "You do not want animals killed or gifts given in worship. **You have made My body ready** as a gift." *(The "gift" was spiritual, emotional and physical redemption)*

Author's Note: It was the Father's will to have Jesus' body made ready (by suffering) as a gift to Him, so that His beloved mankind could be spiritually saved, bodily healed and live a long life.

1 Peter 2:24
He Himself bore our sins in His body on the tree, so that we might die to sins and live for righteousness; by His wounds you have been healed.

PART 5
Spiritual Authority - Casting Out Demons

The Lord is a Warrior; the Lord is His Name.
- Exodus 15:3

And these signs will accompany those who believe: In My Name they will drive out demons ... they will place their hands on sick people, and they will get well.
- Mark 16:17-20

38
Authority in Christ for Victory Over Demonic Oppression and Attack

Author's Note: Having a solid understanding and knowledge of our spiritual authority in Christ is essential when doing spiritual warfare and driving out demons. The victory over our enemy Satan and his army of demons came when Jesus "disarmed the power and authorities, He made a public spectacle of them, triumphing over them by the cross." (Colossians 2:15) Now, through the victory and the finished work of Christ at Calvary, believers in Christ, have complete and total authority over the enemy.

Christians are the Lord's authority on earth. When we command demons to "Go, in Jesus Name," it's as if Jesus Himself were making the command. We are called to fight (1 Timothy 1:18). When we come under demonic attack or when we discern: demonic activity, demonic sickness or demonic strongholds – we are called to fight and command those demonic spirits to flee.

The Old Testament Scriptures that tell us of our victory over our enemies are absolutely just as powerful and applicable for us today as they were in Old Testament times. The only difference is our enemy today is not "flesh and blood (people), but against the rulers, against the authorities, against the powers of this dark world and against spiritual forces of evil in heavenly realms (Satan and his demons)." – Ephesians 6:12

2 Samuel 22:41
You made my enemies *(Satan and demons)* turn their backs in flight, and I destroyed my foes.

Author's Note: Give yourselves totally to God. Stand against the devil, and he will flee from you in terror. - James 4:7

Authority in Christ for Victory Over Demonic Oppression and Attack

Psalm 18:39
You armed me with strength *(authority in Christ)* for battle; **You made my adversaries bow at my feet**.

Author's Note: At the Name of Jesus every demon will bow in submission. – Philippians 2:10

Psalm 44:5
Through You (Jesus) we push back our enemies; **through Your Name *(Jesus)* we trample our foes *(demons)***.

Author's Note: Jesus gave you authority **to trample** on demons and to overcome all the power of Satan; nothing will harm you. – Luke 10:19

Psalm 89:23
I *(the Lord)* will crush his foes before him and strike down his adversaries.

Author's Note: Jesus will crush Satan under your feet. - Romans 16:20

Psalm 91:13
You will tread upon the lion and the cobra; **you will trample the great lion and the serpent** *(devil)*.

Author's Note: In spiritual warfare with demons you are more then conquerors through Jesus. – Romans 8:37

Psalm 108:13
With God we will gain the victory, and He will trample down our enemies.

Author's Note: We overcome Satan and his power by the precious blood of Jesus and the word of our testimony. – Revelation 12:11

Authority in Christ for Victory Over Demonic Oppression and Attack

Psalm 118:7
The LORD is with me; He is my helper. **I will look in triumph on my enemies** *(demons)*.

Author's Note: Jesus disarmed all demons; He made a public spectacle of them, triumphing over them by the cross, so that we could triumph over demons through Him. - Colossians 2:15

Isaiah 54:17
"no weapon forged against you will prevail ... This is the heritage of the servants of the Lord, and this is their vindication from Me," declares the Lord.

Author's Note: Our faith in Christ and His finished work on the cross ensures that we will overcome our enemy in warfare and get victory. — 1 John 5:4

Zechariah 9:8-9
But **I will defend My house against marauding forces. Never again will an oppressor overrun My people**, for now I am keeping watch. Rejoice greatly, O Daughter of Zion! Shout, Daughter of Jerusalem! **See, your King** *(Jesus)* **comes to you, righteous and having salvation**, gentle and riding on a donkey, on a colt, the foal of a donkey.

Matthew 16:18-19 (The Power New Testament)
And I am saying to you that you are Peter, and upon this rock I will build My congregation and **the gates of hell will not prevail against the congregation**. I will give you the keys of the kingdom of the heavens, and whatever you

Authority in Christ for Victory Over Demonic Oppression and Attack

would bind[1] upon the Earth will already have been bound[1] in the heavens with ongoing effect, and whatever you would loose[2] upon the Earth will already have been loosed[2] in the heavens with ongoing effect.

1. Bind – is a Hebrew idiom meaning forbid.
2. Loose – is a Hebrew idiom meaning permit. – *The Power New testament* by William J. Morford

Mark 3:14-15
He appointed twelve--designating them apostles --that they might be with Him and that He might send them out to preach and to **have authority to drive out demons**.

Luke 10:17-19
The seventy-two returned with joy and said, "Lord, even the demons submit to us in Your Name." He replied, "I saw Satan fall like lightning from heaven. **I have given you authority to trample on snakes and scorpions and to overcome all the power of the enemy**; nothing will harm you.

Romans 8:37
No, in all these things we are more than conquerors through Him who loved us.

Romans 16:20a
The God of peace will soon crush Satan under your feet.

2 Corinthians 2:14
But thanks be to God, Who always leads us in triumphal procession in Christ and through us spreads everywhere the fragrance of the knowledge of Him.

Authority in Christ for Victory Over Demonic Oppression and Attack

2 Corinthians 10:3-4
For though we live in the world, we do not wage war as the world does. The weapons we fight with are not the weapons of the world. On the contrary, **they have divine power to demolish strongholds** *(demonic strongholds)*.

Ephesians 1:19-21
and **His incomparably great power for us who believe. That power is like the working of His mighty strength**, which He exerted in Christ when He raised Him from the dead and seated Him at His right hand in the heavenly realms, **far above all rule and authority, power and dominion**, and every title that can be given, not only in the present age but also in the one to come.

Ephesians 2:6
And God raised us up with Christ and **seated us with Him** in heavenly realms in Christ Jesus,

Author's Note: We sit on the chair of authority with Him.

Colossians 2:9-10
For in Christ all the fullness of the Deity lives in bodily form, and **you have been given fullness** *(full authority)* **in Christ, who is the head over every power** *(demonic power)* **and authority** *(demonic authority)*.

1 John 3:8b
The reason the Son of God appeared was to destroy the devil's work.

1 John 5:4 (NLT)
For every child of God defeats this evil world, and we achieve this victory through our faith.

39
Healed From Sickness and Conditions Caused By Evil Spirits

Matthew 9:32-33a
While they were going out, a man who **was demon-possessed and could not talk** was brought to Jesus. And when **the demon was driven out**, the man who was mute spoke.

Author's Note: Muteness can be a spirit that needs to be driven out.

Matthew 12:22
Then they brought Him a **demon-possessed man who was blind and mute, and Jesus healed him**, so that he could both talk and see.

Author's Note: Blindness and muteness can be a spirit that needs to be driven out.

Matthew 15:22, 28
A Canannite woman from that vicinity came to Him, crying out, "Lord, Son of David, have mercy on me! My daughter is suffering terribly from demon-possession. ... Then Jesus answered, "Woman you have great faith! Your request is granted." And her daughter was healed from that very hour.

Author's Note: Through Jesus we can drive out demons from a distance.

Matthew 17:15a, 18
"Lord have mercy on my son," he said. "**He has seizures and is suffering greatly. ... Jesus rebuked the demon**, and it came out of the boy, and he was healed from that moment.

Author's Note: Epilepsy or a like sickness can be a spirit that needs to be driven out.

Healed From Sickness and Conditions Caused By Evil Spirits

Mark 9:25
When Jesus saw that the crowd was running to the scene, He rebuked the evil spirit. "You deaf and mute spirit," He said, **"I command you, come out of him and never enter him again."**

Author's Note: Deafness and muteness can be a spirit that needs to be rebuked and driven out and through Jesus we can forbid any return of demons.

Luke 4:38b-39a
Now Simon's mother-in-law was suffering from a high fever, and they asked Jesus to help her. So **He bent over her and rebuked the fever, and it left her**.

Author's Note: Fevers can be a spirit that needs to rebuked and driven out.

Luke 13:11-13
and a woman was there who had been **crippled by a spirit** for eighteen years. She was bent over and could not straighten up at all. When Jesus saw her, He called her forward and said to her, **"Woman, you are set free from your infirmity."** Then He put His hands on her, and immediately she straightened up and praised God.

Acts 5:16
Crowds gathered also from the towns around Jerusalem, bringing their sick and those tormented by evil spirits, and **all of them were healed**.

Healed From Sickness and Conditions Caused By Evil Spirits

Acts 10:38
how God anointed Jesus of Nazareth with the Holy Spirit and power, and how He went around doing good and **healing all who were under the power of the devil**, because God was with Him.

Author's Note: You will do the same things Jesus did.
– John 14:12

Acts 16:16a, 18b
Once when we were going to a place of prayer, we were met by a slave girl who had a spirit by which she could predict the future. ... Finally Paul became so troubled that he turned around and said to the spirit, "In the Name of Jesus Christ I command you to come out of her!" At that moment the spirit left her.

Author's Note: All occult activity (fortunetelling, magic practices, spiritism, or false religious cults and teachings) are demonic and the evil spirits behind it can be bound and driven out.

Colossians 1:13
For He has rescued us from the dominion of darkness and brought us into the kingdom of the Son He loves,

40
You Will Heal the Sick and Drive Out Demons

"Christ planned to carry out His healing ministry during His absence by means of the whole Church, which is His body, not through an obscure member of that body. He said, "These signs will accompany **THOSE** (the Church) who believe, not "him" – the individual. It was not the faith of a lone or solitary evangelist but that of a Spirit-filled church as a whole which brought healing to all the sick in the streets of Jerusalem after Christ had gone away, and had sent His successor, the Holy Spirit."
- *Christ The Healer* by F.F. Bosworth

Matthew 10:1
He called His twelve disciples to Him and **gave them authority to drive out evil spirits and to heal every disease and sickness**.

Author's Note: God has given all Christians His authority to drive out demons and heal sickness. – John 14:12

Matthew 10:7-8
As you go, preach this message: The kingdom of heaven is near.' **Heal the sick, raise the dead, cleanse those who have leprosy, drive out demons**. Freely you have received, freely give.

Mark 6:13
They *(the Disciples)* **drove out many demons** and anointed many sick people with oil and healed them.

Mark 16:17-18, 20
And **these signs will accompany those who believe**: In My Name *(Jesus Christ)* they will drive out demons; they will speak in new tongues; they will pick up snakes with their

You Will Heal the Sick and Drive Out Demons

hands; and when they drink deadly poison, it will not hurt them at all; **they will place their hands on sick people, and they will get well.**" ... Then the disciples went out and preached everywhere, and the Lord worked with them and **confirmed His Word by the signs that accompanied it**.

Luke 6:17-18
...a great number of people from all over ... had come to hear Him *(Jesus)* and to be healed of their diseases. **Those troubled by evil spirits were cured**,

Luke 8:21
He *(Jesus)* replied, "My mother and brothers are those who hear God's Word and **put it into practice**."

Author's Note: "Practice" healing the sick, raising the dead, cleansing those who have leprosy and driving out demons.

Luke 9:1-2
When Jesus had called the Twelve together, **He gave them power and authority to drive out all demons and to cure diseases, and He sent them** out to preach the kingdom of God and **to heal the sick**.

Luke 10:8-9
When **you** enter a town and are welcomed, eat what is set before you. **Heal the sick who are there** and tell them, 'The kingdom of God is near you.'

John 14:12
"I *(Jesus)* tell you the truth, **anyone who has faith in Me will do what I have been doing**. He will do even greater things than these, because I am going to the Father."

You Will Heal the Sick and Drive Out Demons

Acts 4:29-30
Now, Lord, consider their threats and **enable Your servants to speak Your Word with great boldness. Stretch out Your hand to heal and perform miraculous signs and wonders** through the Name of Your Holy Servant Jesus."

Acts 8:6-7
When the crowds heard Philip and saw the miraculous signs he did, they all paid close attention to what he said. With shrieks, evil spirits came out of many, and many paralytics and cripples were healed.

Acts 13:47
For this is what the **Lord has commanded us**: "'I have made you a light for the Gentiles, that you may **bring salvation** *(health and healing)* to the ends of the earth.'"

Author's Note: The English word "salvation" is translated from the Greek word "soteria" and it means: health, healing, and eternal salvation.

Acts 14:3
So Paul and Barnabas spent considerable time there, speaking boldly for the Lord, who confirmed the message of His grace by **enabling them to do miraculous signs and wonders**.

Acts 14:9-10
He listened to Paul as he was speaking. Paul looked directly at him, saw he had faith to be healed and called out, "Stand up on your feet!" At that, the man jumped up and began to walk.

You Will Heal the Sick and Drive Out Demons

Acts 19:11-12
God did extraordinary miracles through Paul, so that even handkerchiefs and aprons that had touched him were taken to the sick, and **their illnesses were cured and evil spirits left them**.

Author's Note: God wants to use you in the same way.

1 Corinthians 2:4
My message and preaching were not with wise and persuasive words, but **with a demonstration of the Spirit's power**,

Author's Note: The Lord wants to demonstrate His healing power through your message.

Ephesians 2:10
For we are God's workmanship, created in Christ Jesus to do good works, which God prepared in advance for us to do.

Author's Note: Created in Christ Jesus to do good works (healing the sick and raising the dead.)

Hebrews 13:20-21
May the God of peace, who through the blood of the eternal covenant brought back from the dead our Lord Jesus, that great Shepard of the sheep, **equip you with everything good for doing His will**, and may He work in us what is pleasing to Him, through Jesus Christ, to whom be glory for ever and ever. Amen.

Author's Note: Jesus has equipped all Christians to heal the sick and raise the dead.

You Will Heal the Sick and Drive Out Demons

James 5:14-16
Is any one of you sick? He should call the elders of the church to **pray over him and anoint him with oil** in the Name of the Lord. And the prayer offered in faith will make the sick person well; the Lord will raise him up. If he has sinned, he will be forgiven. Therefore confess your sins to each other and **pray for each other so that you may be healed**. **The prayer of a righteous man is powerful and effective**.

Note by F.F. Bosworth: "When after you have been anointed for healing, Satan tells you that you will not recover, like Jesus, say to him, "It is written," "they will get well;" "The Lord will raise him up." Also in this same passage, "in the name of the Lord" means the same as if the Lord, Himself anointed you."

PART 6
Healing the Inner Person

He heals the brokenhearted and binds up their wounds.
- Psalm 147:3

41
Healing For the Broken-Hearted

Nehemiah 8:10b
Do not grieve, for **the joy of the Lord is your strength**.

Psalm 30:5b
weeping may remain for the night, but **rejoicing comes in the morning**.

Psalm 30:11
You turned my wailing into dancing; You removed my sackcloth and **clothed me with joy**,

Psalm 31:24 (NKJ)
Be of good courage, and **He shall strengthen your heart**, all you who hope in the Lord.

Psalm 34:18
The Lord is close to the brokenhearted and saves those who are crushed in spirit.

Psalm 41:4 (AMP)
I said, "Lord, be merciful *and* gracious to me; **heal my inner self**, for I have sinned against You."

Psalm 73:26
My flesh and heart may fail, but **God is the strength of my heart and my portion forever**.

Psalm 119:32
I run in the path of Your commands, for **You have set my heart free**.

Psalm 126:5-6
Those who sow in tears will reap with songs of joy. He who

Healing For the Broken-Hearted

goes out weeping, carrying seed to sow, will return with songs of joy, carrying sheaves with him.

Psalm 147:3
He heals the brokenhearted and binds up their wounds.

Isaiah 35:10b
Gladness and joy will over take them, and sorrow and sighing will flee away.

Isaiah 53:4
Surely He *(Jesus)* took up our infirmities and **carried our sorrows,** yet we considered Him stricken by God, smitten by Him, and afflicted."

Isaiah 57:15
For this is what the high and lofty One says – He Who lives forever, whose Name is holy: "I live in a high and holy place, but also with him who is contrite and lowly in spirit, to **revive the spirit of the lowly and to revive the heart of the contrite**."

Jeremiah 31:13
The maidens will dance and be glad, young men and old as well. I will turn their mourning into gladness; **I will give them comfort and joy instead of sorrow**.

Jeremiah 31:25 (AMP)
For I will [fully] satisfy the weary soul, and **I will replenish every languishing *and* sorrowful person**.

Matthew 5:4
Blessed are those who mourn, for **they will be comforted**.

Healing For the Broken-Hearted

Luke 4:18 (KJ)
The Spirit of the Lord is upon Me, because He hath anointed Me to preach the gospel to the poor; He hath sent Me to **heal the broken-hearted**, to preach deliverance to the captives, recovery of sight to the blind, to **set at liberty them that are bruised**.

Luke 6:21b
Blessed are you who weep now, **for you will laugh**.

John 16:20
"I tell you the truth, you will weep and mourn while the world rejoices. You will grieve, but **your grief will turn to joy**."

42
Healing The Mind

"We need to apply God's weapons against everything that would try to keep our thought patterns and habits in the old way. Strongholds of fear, worry, bitterness, anger, shame, control, etc., need to come down and be replaced by Christ thoughts."
- *The Integrated Approach To Biblical Healing Ministry* by Chester and Betsy Kystra,

"Satan works through the mind, always seeking to implant thoughts that contradict and oppose the Truth of God's Word. This is the reason why we must cast down every ungodly imagination and bring our thoughts in line with the Scriptures (2 Corinthians 10:4-5)."
- *God's Covenant of Healing* by S.J. Hill

"Putting on the new man and having the mind of Christ, includes our thinking and believing what is written, and saying, as He did, "It is written." Remember the "new man" is not governed by the evidence of the senses." – *Christ The Healer* by F. F. Bosworth

Psalm 19:7a
The Law of the Lord is perfect, reviving the soul *(mind)*.
[Meditate on God's word; it's the perfect medicine for healing the mind.]

Author's Note: The English word "soul" is translated from the Hebrew word "nepes" and it means: mind, heart and thoughts.

Psalm 19:14
May the words of my mouth and the meditation of my heart *(imaginations)* be pleasing in Your sight, O Lord, my Rock and my Redeemer.

Author's Note: The English word "heart" is translated from the Hebrew word "leb" and it means: mind, feelings and imagination.

Healing The Mind

Psalm 23:3a
He restores my soul *(mind)*,

Author's Note: The English word "soul" is translated from the Hebrew word "nepes" and it means: mind, heart and thoughts.

Psalm 28:7a (AMP)
The Lord is my Strength and my [impenetrable]Shield;

Author's Note: The Lord will shield your mind from ungodly thoughts.

Psalm 51:10
Create in me a pure heart *(mind and imagination)*, O God, and renew a steadfast spirit within me.

Psalm 140:7
O Sovereign Lord, my strong deliverer, who **shields my head** in the day of battle –

Author's Note: The Lord shields your head (mind, thoughts and attitude) in the day of battle.

Romans 8:5b
…those who live in accordance with the Spirit **have their minds set on what the Spirit desires**.

Romans 12:1
Therefore, I urge you, brothers, in view of God's mercy, to **offer your bodies *(mind and thoughts)* as living sacrifices, holy and pleasing to God**---this is your spiritual act of worship.

Author's Note: The English word "bodies" is translated from the Greek word "soma" and it means: the body as a whole. "Soma" includes your mind and thoughts.

Healing The Mind

Romans 12:2 (NLT)
Don't copy the behavior and customs of this world, but **let God transform you into a new person by changing the way you think**. Then you will learn to know God's will for you, which is good and pleasing and perfect.

Author's Note: Thinking, meditating and exercising your faith in God's Word will transform your life.

1 Corinthians 2:16b
But we have the mind of Christ.

2 Corinthians 5:17
Therefore, if **anyone is in Christ, he is a new creation**; the old has gone, and the new has come!

Author's Note: We have to let go of the old thought patterns, attitudes and beliefs and embrace the new thoughts and attitudes we get with the mind of Christ.

2 Corinthians 10:3-5
For though we live in the world, we do not wage war as the world does. The weapons we fight with are not the weapons of the world. On the contrary, **they have divine power to demolish strongholds**. We demolish arguments and every pretension that sets itself up against the knowledge of God, and **we take captive every thought to make it obedient to Christ**.

Author's Note: The weapons we fight with have divine power to demolish mental and emotional strongholds.

Galatians 3:13
Christ redeemed us from the curse *(mental illness, madness or confusion of mind)* of the Law by becoming

Healing The Mind

a curse for us, for it is written: "Cursed is everyone who is hung on a tree."

Author's Note: Jesus Christ redeemed us from all curses, generational curses and curses of disobedience. The curse of disobedience in Deuteronomy 28:28 would bring madness, blindness and confusion of mind. Appropriate the above promise in Galatians 3:13, in faith, to your mental illness, madness or confusion of mind for your healing. Jesus Christ redeemed you from it, He bore this curse on His body for you and it can't stay.

Ephesians 4:23-24
Be made new in the attitude of your minds; and to put on the new self, created to be like God in true righteousness and holiness.

Ephesians 6:16
In addition to all this, **take up the shield of faith, with which you can extinguish all the flaming arrows** of the evil one.

Author's Note: Take up the shield of faith to extinguish all the flaming arrows of ungodly thoughts, beliefs and attitudes of the evil one.

Ephesians 6:17
Take the helmet of salvation and the sword of the Spirit, which is the Word of God.

Author's Note: Put on the helmet of salvation everyday to protect your mind.

Philippians 4:6-7
Do not be anxious about anything, but in everything, by prayer and petition, with thanksgiving, present your requests to God. And **the peace of God,** which transcends all understanding, **will guard your hearts and your minds in Christ Jesus**.

Healing The Mind

Philippians 4:8-9
Finally, brothers, whatever is true, whatever is noble, whatever is right, whatever is pure, whatever is lovely, whatever is admirable—if anything is excellent or praiseworthy—**think about such things**. Whatever you have learned or received or heard from me, or seen in me—**put it into practice**. And the God of peace will be with you.

Colossians 1:17
He is before all things, and **in Him all things hold together**.

Author's Note: Stay in Jesus and your mind and emotions will hold together.

Colossians 3:1-2
Since, then, you have been raised with Christ, **set your hearts on things above**, where Christ is seated at the right hand of God. **Set your minds on things above**, not on earthly things.

2 Timothy 1:7 (NKJ)
For God has not given us a spirit of fear, but of power, of love and of a **sound mind**.

Hebrews 3:1
Therefore, holy brothers, who share in the heavenly calling, **fix your thoughts on Jesus**, the apostle and high priest whom we confess.

1 Peter 4:1
Therefore, since Christ suffered in His body, **arm yourselves also with the same attitude**, because He Who has suffered in His body is done with sin.

Author's Note: Arm yourselves with the same attitude as Christ and be done with sin.

Healing The Mind

1 Peter 4:7
The end of all things is near. **Therefore be clear minded and self-controlled** so that you can pray.

Author's Note: God would not have commanded us maintain a healthy, clear, and self-controlled mind if it were not possible to do.

43
Break the Bonds of Stress and Anxiety and Walk in the Promise of Peace

"I recommend that all my patients with anxiety quote Scriptures aloud three times a day before meals, meditate on them throughout the day and again quote the scriptures before going to bed.
Pray often, quote scriptures in your prayers and think on the promises of God. Write them down and memorize them.
Put them in places where your can see them – attach sticky notes to your computer or anchor scriptures with magnets on your refrigerator."
- *The Bible Cure For Depression and Anxiety* by Don Colbert, M.D.

Numbers 6:24-26
The LORD bless and keep you; the LORD make His face shine upon you and be gracious to you; **the Lord turn His face towards you and give you peace**.

Numbers 25:12
"Therefore tell him I am making My covenant of peace with him."

1 Samuel 30:6
David was greatly distressed because the men were talking of stoning him; each one was bitter in spirit because of his sons and daughters. **But David found strength in the LORD his God**.

Psalm 29:11
The LORD gives strength to His people; **the Lord blesses His people with peace**.

Break the Bonds of Stress and Anxiety and Walk in the Promise of Peace

Psalm 55:22a
Cast your cares on the LORD and He will sustain you;

Psalm 62:1
My soul finds rest in God alone; my salvation comes from Him.

Psalm 85:8
I will listen to what God the LORD will say; **He promises peace to His people, His saints**

Psalm 94:19
When anxiety was great within me, Your consolation brought joy to my soul.

Ecclesiastes 11:10a
So then, banish anxiety from your heart...

Author's Note: The Lord would not have commanded you to "banish anxiety from your heart" is it were not possible.

Isaiah 26:12
Lord, You establish peace for us; all that we have accomplished You have done for us.

Isaiah 53:5
But He *(Jesus)* was pierced for our transgressions, He was crushed for our iniquities; **the punishment that brought us peace was upon Him**, and by His wounds we are healed.

Isaiah 54:10
"Though the mountains be shaken and the hills removed, yet My unfailing love for you will not be shaken nor My Covenant of peace be removed," says the Lord, Who has compassion on you.

Break the Bonds of Stress and Anxiety and Walk in the Promise of Peace

Isaiah 54:13
All your sons will be taught by the Lord, and **great will be your children's peace**.

Isaiah 55:12
You will go out in joy and be led forth in peace; the mountains and hills will burst into song before you, and all the trees of the field will clap their hands.

Isaiah 60:17b
I will make peace your governor and righteousness your ruler.

Jeremiah 33:6
"Nevertheless, I will bring health and healing to it; **I will heal My people and will let them enjoy abundant peace** and security."

Ezekiel 34:25
I will make a covenant of peace with them and rid the land of wild beasts so that they may live in the desert and sleep in the forests in safety.

Haggai 2:9
"The glory of this present house will be greater than the glory of the former house,' says the LORD Almighty. 'And in this place I will grant peace,' declares the LORD Almighty."

Matthew 11:28-30
"**Come to Me, all you who are weary and burdened, and I will give you rest**. Take My yoke upon you and learn from Me, for I am gentle and humble in heart, and you will find rest for your souls. For My yoke is easy and My burden is light."

Break the Bonds of Stress and Anxiety and Walk in the Promise of Peace

Mark 5:34
He said to her, "Daughter, your faith has healed you. **Go in peace and be freed from your suffering.**"

Luke 1:78-79
because of the tender mercy of our God, by which The Rising Sun will come to us from heaven to shine on those living in darkness and in the shadow of death, **to guide our feet into the path of peace.**"

Luke 2:14
"Glory to God in the highest, and on earth peace to men on whom His favor rests."

John 14:27
Peace I leave with you; My peace I give you. I do not give to you as the world gives. Do not let your hearts be troubled and do not be afraid.

John 16:33
"I have told you these things, so that **in Me you may have peace.** In this world you will have trouble. But take heart! I have overcome the world."

Author's Note: Jesus has overcome the anxiety of the world.

Acts 10:36
You know the message God sent to the people of Israel, telling the good news of **peace through Jesus Christ**, Who is Lord of all.

Romans 14:17
For the kingdom of God is not a matter of eating and drinking, but of righteousness, **peace** and joy in the Holy Spirit,

Break the Bonds of Stress and Anxiety and Walk in the Promise of Peace

1 Corinthians 7:15b
God has called us to live in peace.

Galatians 3:13
Christ redeemed us from the curse *(anxious mind and despairing heart)* **of the law by becoming a curse for us**, for it is written: "Cursed is everyone who is hung on a tree."

Author's Note: Jesus Christ redeemed us from all curses, generational curses and curses of disobedience. The curse of disobedience in Deuteronomy 28:65 would bring an anxious mind, weary eyes with longing, and a dispersing. Appropriate the above promise in Galatians 3:13, in faith, to your anxiety and despairing heart for your healing. Jesus Christ redeemed you from it. He bore this curse on His body for you and it can't stay.

Galatians 5:22
But the fruit of the Spirit is love, joy, **peace**, patience, kindness, goodness, faithfulness,

Ephesians 2:14a
For He *(Jesus)* **himself is our peace...**

Colossians 3:15
Let the peace of Christ rule in your hearts, since as members of one body **you were called to peace**. And be thankful.

2 Thessalonians 3:16
Now may the Lord of peace Himself give you peace at all times and in every way. The Lord be with all of you.

1 Peter 1:2b
Grace and peace be yours in abundance.

1 Peter 5:7
Cast all your anxiety on Him because He cares for you.

44
How to Live in Peace

Psalm 37:11
But the meek will inherit the land and **enjoy great peace**.

Psalm 119:165
Great peace have they who love Your Law, and nothing can make them stumble.

Proverbs 16:7
When a man's ways are pleasing to the LORD, He makes even his enemies live at peace with him.

Isaiah 26:3 (NLT)
You will keep in perfect peace all who trust in You, all whose thoughts are fixed on You!

Isaiah 32:17
The fruit of righteousness will be peace; the effect of righteousness will be quietness and confidence forever.

Isaiah 57:2a
Those who walk uprightly enter into peace;

Jeremiah 6:16
…ask where the good way is, and walk in it, and you will find rest for your souls.

Roman 2:10
but glory, honor and **peace for everyone who does good**: first for the Jew, then for the Gentile.

Romans 8:6
The mind of sinful man is death, but **the mind controlled by the Spirit is life and peace**;

How to Live in Peace

Romans 15:13a
May the God of hope fill you with all joy and peace **as you trust in Him**,

Philippians 4:8-9
Finally, brothers, whatever is true, whatever is noble, whatever is right, whatever is pure, whatever is lovely, whatever is admirable--if anything is excellent or praiseworthy--**think about such things.** Whatever you have learned or received or heard from me, or seen in me--put it into practice. **And the God of peace will be with you.**

2 Peter 1:2
Grace and peace be yours in abundance **through the knowledge of God and of Jesus our Lord**.

45
You've Been Set Free From Fear

Joshua 1:9
Have I not commanded you? Be strong and courageous. Do not be terrified; do not be discouraged, for **the LORD your God will be with you wherever you go**.

Job 5:21-22
You will be protected from the lash of the tongue, and need not fear when destruction comes. You will laugh at destruction and famine, and need not fear the beasts of the earth.

Psalm 3:6
I will not fear the tens of thousands drawn up against me on every side.

Psalm 23:4
Even though I walk through the valley of the shadow of death, **I will fear no evil, for You are with me**; Your rod and Your staff, they comfort me.

Psalm 27:1
The LORD is my light and my salvation - whom shall I fear? **The LORD is the stronghold of my life - of whom shall I be afraid?**

Psalm 34:4
I sought the LORD, and He answered me; He delivered me from all my fears.

Psalm 91:5-7
You will not fear the terror of night, nor the arrow that flies by day, nor the pestilence that stalks in the darkness, nor the plague that destroys at midday. A thousand may fall at your

You've Been Set Free From Fear

side, ten thousand at your right hand, **but it will not come near you**.

Psalm 112:6-7
…a righteous man will be remembered forever. He will have no fear of bad news; his heart is steadfast, trusting in the LORD. His heart is secure, he will have no fear; in the end he will look in triumph on his foes.

Proverbs 1:33
but whoever listens to Me will live in safety and be at ease, **without fear of harm**.

Proverbs 3:24
when you lie down, **you will not be afraid**; when you lie down, your sleep will be sweet.

Proverbs 3:25-26
Have no fear of sudden disaster or of the ruin that overtakes the wicked, **for the LORD will be your confidence and will keep your foot from being snared**.

Isaiah 8:12
"Do not call conspiracy everything these people call conspiracy; do not fear what they fear, and do not dread it."

Isaiah 12:2
Surely God is my salvation; **I will trust and not be afraid**. The LORD, the LORD, is my strength and my song; He has become my salvation."

Isaiah 35:4
say to those with fearful hearts, "Be strong, **do not fear; your God will come**, He will come with vengeance; with divine retribution He will come to save you."

You've Been Set Free From Fear

Isaiah 41:10
So do not fear, for I am with you; do not be dismayed, for I am your God. I will strengthen you and help you; I will uphold you with My righteous right hand.

Isaiah 41:13
"For I am the LORD, your God, Who takes hold of your right hand and says to you, **Do not fear; I will help you**."

Isaiah 43:1-2
But now, this is what the LORD says-- He who created you, O Jacob, He who formed you, O Israel: "**Fear not, for I have redeemed you**; I have summoned you by name; you are mine. When you pass through the waters, I will be with you; and when you pass through the rivers, they will not sweep over you. When you walk through the fire, you will not be burned; the flames will not set you ablaze."

Isaiah 51:12
"I, even I, am He who comforts you. Who are you that you fear mortal men, who are but grass."

Isaiah 54:14
In righteousness you will be established: Tyranny will be far from you; **you will have nothing to fear**. Terror will be far removed; it will not come near you.

Jeremiah 17:7-8
"But **blessed is the man who trusts in the Lord, whose confidence is in Him**. He will be like a tree planted by the water that sends out its roots by the stream. It does not fear when heat comes; its leaves are always green. It has no worries in the year of drought and never fails to bear fruit."

You've Been Set Free From Fear

Mark 5:35-36
While Jesus was still speaking, some men came from the house of Jairus, the synagogue ruler. "Your daughter is dead," they said. "Why bother the Teacher any more?" Ignoring what they said, Jesus told the synagogue ruler, **"Don't be afraid; just believe."**

Romans 8:15
For **you did not receive a spirit that makes you a slave again to fear**, but you received the Spirit of sonship. And by Him we cry, "Abba, Father."

2 Timothy 1:7 (NKJ)
For God has not given us a spirit of fear, but of power, of love and of a sound mind.

Author's Note: Don't tolerate a demonic spirit of fear attempting to control your life. Recognize it for what it is and command it to leave you in Jesus Name.

1 John 4:18a
There is no fear in love. But perfect love drives out fear

Author's Note: Jesus drives out fear.

46
Live a Joy-Filled Life

Job 8:21
He will yet fill your mouth **with laughter** and your lips **with shouts of joy**.

Psalm 4:7
You have **filled my heart with greater joy** than when their grain and new wine abound.

Psalm 16:11
You have made known to me the path of life; **You will fill me with joy in Your presence**, with eternal pleasures at Your right hand.

Psalm 19:8
The precepts of the Lord are right, **giving joy to the heart**. The commands of the Lord are radiant, giving light to the eyes.

Psalm 28:7
The Lord is my strength and my shield; my heart trusts in Him, and I am helped. **My heart leaps for joy** and I give thanks to Him in a song.

Psalm 45:7
You love righteousness and hate wickedness; therefore God, your **God has set you above your companions by anointing you with the oil of joy**.

Psalm 51:12
Restore to me the joy of Your salvation and grant me a willing spirit, to sustain me.

Live a Joy-Filled Life

Psalm 68:3
But may the righteous be glad and rejoice before God; may they be happy and joyful.

Psalm 86:4
Bring joy to Your servant, for to You, O Lord, I lift up my soul.

Psalm 97:11
Light is shed upon the righteous and **joy on the upright in heart**.

Psalm 105:43
He brought out His people with rejoicing, His chosen ones with shouts of joy;

Psalm 118:15
Shouts of joy and victory resound in the tents of the righteous: "The Lord's right hand has done mighty things!"

Psalm 126:3
The Lord has done great things for us, and we are filled with joy.

Isaiah 9:3
You have enlarged the nation and increased their joy; they rejoice before You as people rejoice at the harvest, as men rejoice when dividing the plunder.

Isaiah 12:3
With joy you will draw water from the wells of salvation.

Isaiah 55:12
You will go out in joy and be led forth in peace; the mountains and hills will burst into song before you, and all the trees of the field will clap their hands.

Live a Joy-Filled Life

Isaiah 60:5
Then you will look and be radiant, **your heart will throb and swell with joy**; the wealth of the seas will be brought to you, to you the riches of the nation will come.

Isaiah 65:14a
My servants will sing out of the joy of their hearts,

Luke 6:21b
Blessed are you who weep now, **for you will laugh**.

John 15:11
I have told you this so that **My joy may be in you and that your joy may be complete**.

John 17:13
"I am coming to you now, but I say these things while I am still in the world, **so that they may have the full measure of My joy within them**."

Acts 2:28
'You have made known to me the path of life; **You fill me with joy in Your presence**.'

Acts 13:52
And the disciples were filled with joy and with the Holy Spirit.

Acts 14:17b
He has shown kindness by giving rain from heaven and crops in their seasons; He provides you with plenty of food and **fills your hearts with joy**.

Romans 14:17
For the kingdom of God is not a matter of eating and drinking, but of righteousness, peace and **joy in the Holy Spirit**,

Live a Joy-Filled Life

2 Corinthians 7:4
…in all our troubles **our joy knows no bounds**.

Galatians 5:22
But the fruit of the Spirit is love, **joy,** peace, patience, kindness, goodness, faithfulness,

Philippians 4:4
Rejoice in the Lord always. I will say it again: Rejoice!

1 Thessalonians 5:16
Be joyful always;

1 Peter 1:8
Though you have not seen Him, you love Him; and even though you do not see Him now, **you believe in Him and are filled with an inexpressible and glorious joy**,

PART 7
Healing the Spirit: Eternal Life

And this is the testimony: God has given us eternal life, and **this life is in His Son**. He who has the Son has life; he who does not have the Son of God does not have life.
- 1 John 5:11-12

47
Eternal Life is Through Jesus Christ

John 3:16
For God so loved the world that He gave His One and only Son, that **whoever believes in Him** shall not perish but have eternal life.

John 3:36
Whoever believes in the Son has eternal life, but whoever rejects the Son will not see life, for God's wrath remains on him.

John 5:24
I tell you the truth, **whoever hears My Word and believes Him Who sent Me has eternal life** and will not be condemned; he has crossed over from death to life.

John 6:40
For My Father's Will is that everyone who looks to the Son and believes in Him shall have eternal life, and I will raise him up at the last day.

John 6:47
I tell you the truth, **he who believes has everlasting life**.

John 10:9a
I *(Jesus)* am the gate *(to eternal life)*; whoever enters through Me will be saved.

John 10:27-28
My sheep listen to My voice; I know them, and they follow Me. I give them eternal life, and **they shall never perish**; no one can snatch them out of My hand.

Eternal Life is Through Jesus Christ

John 11:25-26
Jesus said to her, "I am the resurrection and the life. He who believes in Me will live, even though he dies; and whoever lives and believes in Me will never die. Do you believe this?"

John 14:6
Jesus answered, "I am the Way and the Truth and the Life. **No one comes to the Father except through Me.**"

John 14:23
Jesus replied, "If anyone loves Me, he will obey My teaching. My father will love him, and We will come to him and make Our home with him."

Acts 4:12
Salvation is found in no one else, for there is no other Name (Jesus) under heaven given to men by which we must be saved.

Romans 6:23
For the wages of sin is death *(eternal hell)*, but the gift of God is eternal life in Christ Jesus our Lord.

Romans 10:9-10
That if you **confess** with your mouth, "Jesus is Lord," and **believe** in your heart that God raised Him from the dead, **you will be saved *(given eternal life)*.** For it is with your heart that you believe and are justified, and it is with your mouth that you confess and are saved.

Galatians 3:22
But the Scripture declares that the whole world is a prisoner of sin, so that what was promised *(eternal life)*, **being given through faith in Jesus Christ**, might be given to those who believe.

Eternal Life is Through Jesus Christ

Ephesians 2:8-9
For it is by grace you have been saved *(given eternal life)*, through faith - and this not from yourselves, it is the gift of God - not by works, so that no one can boast.

Hebrews 5:9
and, once made perfect, He *(Jesus)* became the source of eternal salvation for all who obey Him

Hebrews 7:24-25
but because Jesus lives forever, He has a permanent priesthood. Therefore **He is able to save completely those who come to God through Him**, because He always lives to intercede for them.

1 John 5:11-12
And this is the testimony: God has given us eternal life, and this life is in His Son. **He who has the Son has life** *(eternal life)*; he who does not have the Son of God does not have life.

48
You Must Turn from Sin (Repent) to Receive Eternal Life

The Bible clearly states that repentance is critical to receiving eternal life. When a person receives Christ as his personal Lord and Savior, the fruit that MUST come out of that new relationship with God is repentance (changing your mind and purpose, amending your ways, turning around, and turning to God.)

Living a lifestyle of sin (not turning from sin - repenting) would be a serious miscalculation (with a horrifying eternal consequence) of what God commands of those that confess Jesus as Lord and Savior. By repenting you prove to God that you love Him and are serious about your relationship with Him.

The Lord Jesus made this issue clear in Matthew 7:20-23: "Thus, by their fruit you will recognize them. Not everyone who says to me, 'Lord, Lord,' will enter the kingdom of heaven, but only he who does the will of My Father who is in heaven. Many will say to Me on that day (judgment day), 'Lord, Lord, did we not prophesy in Your Name, and in Your Name drive out demons and perform many miracles?' Then I will tell them plainly, 'I never new you. Away from me, you evil doers!'"

Ezekiel 18:32
For I take no pleasure in the death *(spiritual death--eternal hell)* of anyone, declares the Sovereign Lord. **Repent and live!**

Luke 13:3 (AMP)
I tell you, No; but unless you repent **(change your mind for the better and heartily amend your ways, with**

You Must Turn from Sin (Repent) to Receive Eternal Life

abhorrence of your past sins), you too will all likewise perish *and* be eternally lost.

Luke 24:46-47
He *(Jesus)* told them, "This is what is written: The Christ will suffer and rise from the dead on the third day, and repentance and forgiveness of sins will be preached in His Name to all nations, beginning at Jerusalem.

Acts 17:30-31
In the past God overlooked such ignorance, but **now He commands all people everywhere to repent**. For He has set a day when He will judge the world with justice by the Man He has appointed. He has given proof of this to all men by raising Him from the dead.

Acts 20:21
I have declared to both Jews and Greeks that **they must turn to God in repentance** and have faith in our Lord Jesus.

2 Peter 3:9
The Lord is not slow in keeping His promise, as some understand slowness. He is patient with you, **not wanting anyone to perish, but everyone to come to repentance**.

1 John 3:6
No one who lives in Him keeps on sinning. No one who continues to sin has either seen Him or known Him.

49
Steps to Salvation and Eternal Life

1. God created you as an eternal being. You are an eternal being with the free will to make the choice that will determine where you will spend the rest of your eternal life:
"This day I call heaven and earth as witnesses against you that I set before you life and death, blessing and curses. Now choose life." – Deuteronomy 30:19

And this is the testimony: God has given us eternal life, and this life is in His Son. He who has the Son has life; he who does not have the Son of God does not have life. – 1 John 5:11-12

2. Being saved is believing in Jesus for eternal life:
"For God so loved the world that He gave His One and only Son, that whoever believes in Him shall not perish but have eternal life." – John 3:16

3. The reason we must be saved is because we are all sinners. Our sin separates us from God and eternal life:
"for *all* have sinned and fall short of the glory of God." – Romans 3:23

"For the wages of sin is death, but the gift of God is eternal life in Christ Jesus our Lord." – Romans 6:23

"If we confess our sins, He is faithful and just and will forgive us our sins and purify us from all unrighteousness." – 1 John 1:9

Steps to Salvation and Eternal Life

4. You cannot earn salvation and you cannot do it on your own. It is God's gift to you:
"God saved you by His special favor when you believed. And you can't take credit for this; it is a gift from God. Salvation is not a reward for the good things we have done, so none of us can brag about it." – Ephesians 2:8-9 (NLT)

5. Being saved is receiving Jesus as your Lord (Master) and committing yourself to follow His Word:
"That if you confess with your mouth, "Jesus is Lord," and believe in your heart that God raised Him from the dead, you will be saved. For it is with your heart that you believe and are justified, and it is with your mouth that you confess and are saved." – Romans 10: 9-10

"We know that we have come to know Him if we obey His commands." – 1 John 2:3

6. If you are ready to make this life-changing commitment to receive salvation than pray this simple prayer:

"God I come to You in the Name of Jesus. I ask You to come into my life. I confess with my mouth that Jesus is my Lord, and I believe in my heart that You have raised Him from the dead. Please forgive me of my sins. I turn my back on sin and renounce all religions. I am now a child of God."

7. If you prayed to receive Salvation through Jesus Christ. You should confess to somebody that Jesus has saved you and He's given you eternal life:
Jesus did not let him, but said, "Go home to your family and tell them how much the Lord has done for you, and how He has had mercy on you.'" – Mark 5:19

Steps to Salvation and Eternal Life

8. You need to read your Bible and be trained in God's Word to grow your faith in God:
"Consequently, faith comes from hearing the message, and the message is heard through the Word of Christ."
– Romans 10:17

9. Ask God to give you His vision and great plan for your new life in Christ and then pour your life into it:
"For I know the plans I have for you, declares the Lord, plans to prosper you and not harm you, plans to give you hope and a future." – Jeremiah 29:11

"In the last days, God says, I will pour out my Spirit on all people. Your sons and daughters will prophesy, your young men will see visions, your old men will dream dreams. Even on My servants, both men and women, I will pour out My Spirit in those days, and they will prophesy." - Acts 2:17-18

10. Settle for nothing less then fulfilling your destiny in Christ:
"In Him we were also chosen, having been predestined according to the plan of Him who works out everything in conformity with the purpose of His will, – Ephesians 1:11

PART 8
Major Obstacles To Receiving Healing

Some became fools through their rebellious ways and suffered affliction because of their iniquities.
- Psalm 107:17

50
Lack of Faith Will Hinder and Prevent Healing and the Miraculous

"God is just as faithful to one Promise as to another. Therefore it is equally as foolish to doubt God's Promise to heal because of pain or any disagreeable feeling, as it is to question Christ's second coming because of these things. Since God has provided and promised healing, we should dismiss from our minds the slightest thought of failing to be healed." – *Christ The Healer* by F.F. Bosworth

"When appropriating the healing Promises, God warns us, in the case of Peter, to never look at our circumstances and our feelings. The waves were just as high when Peter walked perfectly on the water as when he sank. While he did not look at them, they could not hinder him; but the minute he looked at them, he doubted and went down. The wind also was just as great when Peter walked perfectly, as when he sank. When he did not pay attention to it, it could not hinder him. God here teaches us that if we are occupied with looking and feeling, instead of Him and His Word, we will lose all He offers. On the other hand, by steadfastly refusing to see anything but God and what He says, we shall have and keep everything that He says He has given us."
- Mrs. C. Nuzum

Numbers 14:33
Your children will be shepherd's here for forty years, **suffering for your unfaithfulness**, until the last of your bodies lie in the desert.

Author's Note: The generation of Israelites that came out of Egypt, were not able to enter into the Promises of God because of their lack of faith. "These things happened to them as examples and were written down as warnings for us on whom the fulfillment of the ages has come." – 1 Corinthians 10:11

Lack of Faith Will Hinder and Prevent Healing and the Miraculous

2 Chronicles 16:12-13
In the thirty-ninth year of his reign Asa was afflicted with a disease in his feet. Though his disease was severe, **even in his illness he did not seek the Lord, but only from the physicians**. Then in the forty-first year of his reign Asa died and rested with his fathers.

Psalm 78:20-22
When he struck the rock, water gushed out, and streams flowed abundantly. But can He also give us food? *(But can He also heal my body?)* Can He supply meat for His people? *(Can He supply good health for His people?)* When the Lord heard them, He was very angry; His fire broke out against Jacob, and His wrath rose against Israel, for **they did not believe in God or trust in His deliverance**.

Isaiah 7:9b
If you do not stand firm in your faith, **you will not stand at all**.

Matthew 13:57-58
And they took offense at Him. But Jesus said to them, "Only in His hometown and in His own house is a prophet without honor." And **He did not do many miracles there because of their lack of faith**.

Matthew 17:15-20
"Lord, have mercy on my son," he said. "He has seizures and is suffering greatly. He often falls into the fire or into the water. **I brought him to Your disciples, but they could not heal him." "O unbelieving and perverse generation," Jesus replied**, "how long shall I stay with you? How long shall I put up with you? Bring the boy here to Me." Jesus

Lack of Faith Will Hinder and Prevent Healing and the Miraculous

rebuked the demon, and it came out of the boy, and he was healed from that moment. Then the disciples came to Jesus in private and asked, "Why couldn't we drive it out?" He replied, **"Because you have so little faith."**

Mark 6:5-6
He could not do any miracles there, except lay His hands on a few sick people and heal them. And **He was amazed at their lack of faith**. Then Jesus went around teaching from village to village.

Mark 9:24 (NLT)
The father instantly cried out, "I do believe, but help me overcome my unbelief!"

"Unbelief is a sin. Confess to God your unbelief and count on Him for deliverance from it, the same as for any other sin. Unbelief is wicked and unrighteous because it hinders and sets aside the divine program which consists of all God has promised to do in response to faith."
- *Gems of Truth on Divine Healing*

Luke 8:12-13
"Those along the path are the ones who hear, and the devil comes to take away the word from their hearts, **so that they may not believe and be saved *(healed)*.** Those on the rock are the ones who receive the Word with joy when they hear it, but they have no root. They believe for a while, but in the time of testing they fall away."

1 Timothy 4:1
The Spirit clearly says that in later times some will abandon the faith *(faith for healing)* and following deceiving spirits and things taught by demons.

Author's Note: This is a warning for the church today. Never in all of church history, certainly in the western world church, have such

Lack of Faith Will Hinder and Prevent Healing and the Miraculous

huge portions of the church and whole denominations abandoned, and teach against, faith in the finished work of Christ for healing. And many of those that say they believe God for healing, are really double-minded. They run to the physicians and medicine and vitamins as their first line of defense against sickness. It's the Devil, the spirit of doubt and un-belief, that doesn't want you to believe and act upon what God says.

Hebrews 3:18-19
And to whom did God swear that they will never enter His rest if not to those who disobeyed? **So we see they were not able to enter, because of their unbelief**.

Author's Note: "they were not able to enter (enter into the Promises of God), because of their unbelief."

Hebrews 4:2
For we also have had the gospel preached to us, just as they did; but **the message they heard was of no value to them, because those who heard it did not combine it with faith**.

Hebrews 10:37-38
For in just a very little while, "He who is coming will come and will not delay. But my righteous one will live by faith. And if he shrinks back, I will not be pleased with him." But we are not those who shrink back and are destroyed, but of those who believe and are saved *(healed)*.

James 1:5-7
...ask God, who gives generously to all without finding fault, and it will be given to him. **But when he asks, he must believe and not doubt**, because he who doubts is like a wave of the sea, blown and tossed by the wind. That man should not think he will receive anything from the Lord;

Author's Note: "But when he asks (asks for healing), he must believe and not doubt,"

51
Sin and a Lifestyle of Disobedience Will Hinder and Prevent Healing, and Bring on Sickness and Demonic Oppression

Author's Note: Satan and demons have been legally disarmed and stripped of authority. Their rights to afflict Christians have been revoked. But demons don't play fair; they are relentless and they will continue to harass and attack. Their mission is to steal and kill and destroy. But every believer in the Lord Jesus Christ has authority to live victoriously over the enemy, unless they give the enemy the legal right to their lives. **Sin in our lives gives the enemy legal right**. It opens the door and it gives the enemy free and legal access to come in and fulfill his mission (to steal, kill and destroy).

The only safe position is a clean and obedient life. Jesus makes this clear in John 14:30, "for the prince of this world is coming. He has no hold on Me." "Do not give the devil a foothold." (Ephesians 4:24). "Your enemy the devil prowls around like a roaring lion looking for someone to devour." (1 Peter 5:8)

"Remember, healing isn't unconditionally promised to all who merely confess Christ as Savior. Only those who lovingly obey God's Word can expect to walk in God's Covenant of healing! It is said in Psalm 25:10 (NKJ) - All the paths of the LORD *are* mercy and truth, to such as **keep** His covenant and His testimonies." – *God's Covenant of Healing* by S.J. Hill

Genesis 4:6-11
Then the Lord said to Cain, Why are you angry? Why is your face down cast? If you do right, will you not be accepted? But if you do not do what is right,

Sin and a Lifestyle of Disobedience Will Hinder and Prevent Healing, and Bring on Sickness and Demonic Oppression

sin is crouching at your door; it desires to have you, but you must master it. ...Then the Lord said ... Your brother's blood cries out to me from the ground. **Now you are under a curse** (sin and sickness)

Author's Note: Satan is at the door, of sin, waiting to devour the person that opens that opens it.

Deuteronomy 28:58-61
If you do not carefully follow all the Words of this Law, which are written in this Book, and do not revere this glorious and awesome Name the LORD your God the LORD will send fearful plagues on you and your descendants, harsh and prolonged disasters, and severe and lingering illnesses. He will bring upon you all the diseases of Egypt that you dreaded, and they will cling to you. The LORD will also bring on you every kind of sickness and disaster not recorded in this Book of the Law, until you are destroyed.

2 Chronicles 7:14
if My people, who are called by My Name, **will humble themselves and pray and seek My face and turn from their wicked ways, then will I hear from heaven** and will forgive their sin and will heal their land.

Psalm 32:3-5
When I kept silent, my bones wasted away through my groaning all day long. For day and night Your hand was heavy upon me; my strength was sapped as in the heat of summer. Then I acknowledged my sin to You and did not cover up my iniquity. I said, "I will confess my transgressions to the Lord"- and You forgave the guilt of my sin.

Sin and a Lifestyle of Disobedience Will Hinder and Prevent Healing, and Bring on Sickness and Demonic Oppression

Psalm 38:3
Because of Your wrath there is no health in my body; my bones have no soundness **because of my sin**.

Psalm 38:5-7
My wounds fester and are loathsome **because of my sinful folly.** I am bowed down and brought very low; all day long I go about mourning. My back is filled with searing pain; there is no health in my body.

Psalm 39:11 (CE)
You punish us severely because of our sins. Like a moth, you destroy what we treasure most. We are as frail as a breath.

Psalm 41:4
I said, "O Lord, have mercy on me; heal me, for I have sinned against You."

Psalm 55:19
God, Who is enthroned forever, will hear them and **afflict them-- men who never change their ways** and have no fear of God.

Psalm 66:18
If I had **cherished sin in my heart**, the Lord would not have listened;

Author's Note: "The Lord would not have listened" to my prayers for healing.

Psalm 106:43
Many times He delivered them, but they were bent on rebellion and **they wasted away in their sin**.

Sin and a Lifestyle of Disobedience Will Hinder and Prevent Healing, and Bring on Sickness and Demonic Oppression

Psalm 107:17
Some became **fools through their rebellious ways and suffered affliction because of their iniquities**.

Psalm 119:67
Before I was afflicted I went astray, but now I obey Your Word.

Proverbs 6:27-29
Can a man scoop fire into his lap without his clothes being burned? Can a man walk on hot coals without his feet being scorched? So is he who sleeps with another man's wife; no one who touches her will go unpunished.

Proverbs 14:30
A heart at peace gives life to the body, but **envy rots the bones**.

Proverbs 28:13
He who conceals his sins does not prosper (have health), but whoever confesses and renounces them finds mercy.

Author's Note: The English word "prosper" is translated from the Hebrew word "dasen" and it means: gives health and fully satisfied.

Isaiah 1:5-6
Why should you be beaten anymore? Why do you persist in rebellion? Your whole head is injured, your whole heart afflicted. From the sole of your foot to the top of your head there is no soundness - only wounds and welts and open sores, not cleansed or bandaged or soothed with oil.

Sin and a Lifestyle of Disobedience Will Hinder and Prevent Healing, and Bring on Sickness and Demonic Oppression

Isaiah 59:2
But your iniquities have separated you from your God; your sins have hidden His face from you, **so that He will not hear** *(hear your healing prayer).*

Author's note: It is a serious miscalculation to think a person can live an unholy lifestyle and claim the covenant blessings of God as an inherited right at the same time.

Jeremiah 2:19
"Your wickedness will punish you; your backsliding will rebuke you. Consider then and realize how evil and bitter it is for you when you forsake the Lord your God and have no awe of Me," declares the Lord, the Lord Almighty.

Ezekiel 18:30
"Therefore, O house of Israel, I will judge you, each according to his ways, declares the Sovereign Lord. Repent! Turn away from all your offenses; then sin will not be your downfall."

Hosea 4:6a
My people are destroyed from lack of knowledge.

Author's Note: We need to ask the Holy Spirit to give us knowledge of any sin in our life. Un-repented sin or un-confessed sin leaves an open door to the enemy and gives him a legal right to oppress us or afflict us.

Hosea 6:1
"**Come let us return to the LORD**. He has torn us to pieces but He will heal us; He has injured us but He will bind up our wounds.

Sin and a Lifestyle of Disobedience Will Hinder and Prevent Healing, and Bring on Sickness and Demonic Oppression

Matthew 15:4
"For God said, 'Honor your father and mother' and 'Anyone who curses his father and mother must be put to death.'"

Matthew 18:7
"Woe to the world because of the things that cause people to sin!" Such things must come, but woe to the man through whom they come!"

John 5:14
Later Jesus found him at the temple and said to him, "See you are well again. **Stop sinning or something worse may happen to you.**"

Acts 3:19 (AMP)
So repent [change your mind and purpose]; turn around and return [to God], that your sins may be erased [blotted out, wiped clean], **that times of refreshing** [of recovering from the effects of heat, of reviving with fresh air] **may come from the presence of the Lord**;

Acts 15:29
You are to abstain from food sacrificed to idols, from blood, from meat of strangled animals and from sexual immorality. **You will do well to avoid these things**.

Author's Note: Since this is true, then the reverse is true. If you do not abstain from these things then it will not do you well.

1 Corinthians 11:28-30
A man ought to examine himself before he eats the bread and drinks of the cup. For anyone who eats and drinks without recognizing the body of the Lord eats and drinks

Sin and a Lifestyle of Disobedience Will Hinder and Prevent Healing, and Bring on Sickness and Demonic Oppression

judgment on himself. That is why many among you are weak and sick, and a number of you have fallen asleep.

Galatians 6:7-8a
Do not be deceived: God cannot be mocked. A man reaps what he sows. The one who sows to please his sinful nature, from that nature will reap destruction;

1 Peter 3:7
Husbands, in the same way be considerate as you live with your wives, and treat them with respect as the weaker partner and as heirs with you of the gracious gift of life, **so that nothing will hinder your prayers**.

Author's Note: "…So that nothing will hinder your prayers (prayers for healing)."

Revelation 2:20-23
"Nevertheless, I have this against you: You tolerate that women Jezebel, who calls herself a prophetess. By her teaching she misleads My servants into sexual immorality and the eating of food sacrificed to idols. **I have given her time to repent of her immorality, but she is unwilling. So I will cast her on a bed of suffering, and make those who commit adultery with her suffer intensely, unless they repent of her ways**. I will strike her children dead. Then all the churches will know that I am He who searches hearts and minds, and I will repay each of you according to your deeds."

52
Ungodly, Negative Thoughts and Attitude Can Produce a Sick and Oppressed Life

"An attitude is a choice. A person can choose to have a negative attitude, or he can choose to have a positive attitude. You choose to be angry, bitter, resentful, fearful or ashamed. These negative attitudes eventually affect our health and allow diseases to take root in our bodies. Resentment and un-forgiveness are commonly associated with arthritis, whereas fear is commonly associated with ulcers, and anger is very commonly associated with heart disease. These are deadly emotions. If they are not taken out of us through the Word of God or with the help of a trained professional, they can eventually lead to disease."
- *The Bible Cure For Depression and Anxiety*, by Don Colbert, M.D.

"It's imperative that we change our way of thinking and bring our thoughts into conformity to the Word of God. We dare not allow our thoughts to dwell continually on our physical condition for this will only make matters worse. The majority of people today are much to inclined to talk about their illnesses and discuss their symptoms with others. Little do they realize the harm they are doing to themselves by keeping their minds filled with thoughts of sickness rather then filling their minds with the promises of God. If the mind is always thinking about some physical ailment, one can hardly expect the condition to improve and the body to mend."
- *God's Covenant of Healing* by S.J. Hill

Job 3:25
What I feared has come upon me; what I dreaded has happened to me.

Ungodly, Negative Thoughts and Attitude Can Produce a Sick and Oppressed Life

Proverbs 15:15 (AMP)
All the days of the desponding *and* afflicted are made evil [by anxious thoughts and forebodings], but he who has a glad heart has a continual feast [regardless of the circumstances.]

Proverbs 17:22
A cheerful heart is good medicine, but **a crushed spirit dries up the bones**.

Proverbs 23:7 (NKJ)
for as he *(a person)* **thinks in his heart, so is he**.

Author's Note: This Scripture is a huge warning about thinking sick and diseased thoughts toward ourselves. "For as he thinks he's sick and diseased so is he."

Matthew 7:17
Likewise, every good tree bears good fruit, but **a bad tree bears bad fruit**. A good tree can not bear bad fruit, and **a bad tree can not bear good fruit**.

Author's Note: "every bad tree (sick and ungodly thoughts or negative thinking patterns) bears bad fruit (sick, negative and oppressed life.")

Matthew 15:18
"But the things that come out of the mouth come from the heart, and these make a man 'unclean.' For out of the heart comes evil thoughts, murder, sexual immorality, theft, false testimony, slander. These are what make a man unclean;"

Ungodly, Negative Thoughts and Attitude Can Produce a Sick and Oppressed Life

Matthew 12:33
"Make a tree (your thoughts) good and its fruit *(life)* will be good *(healed)*, or **make a tree *(your thoughts)* bad and its fruit *(life)* will be bad *(sick)***, for a tree is recognized by its fruit."

Luke 6:45
"The good man brings good things *(healed and healthy life)* out of the good stored up in his heart *(thoughts and mind)*, and the evil man brings evil things *(a sick life)* out of the evil stored up in his heart *(thoughts and mind)*…"

Author's Note: The English word "heart" is translated from the Greek word "kardia" and it means: thoughts and mind.

Romans 6:12
Therefore do not let sin reign in your mortal body *(thoughts and mind)* so that you obey its evil desires.

Romans 8:5a
Those who live according to the sinful nature **have their minds set** on what that nature desires;

Author's Note: You will eventually live out in life according to what your mind is set on.

Ephesians 4:22
You were taught, with regard to your former way of life, to put off your old self, which is **being corrupted by its deceitful desires**;

Author's Note: "Put off your old self (old negative thoughts)," which will corrupt your life.

53
Unforgiveness Will Hinder and Prevent Healing, Invite Sickness and Open the Door to Demonic Oppression

"In God's economy, forgiveness is the principle activity and heart attitude needed to pave the way for freedom. It is the key to freedom. As long as unforgiveness is present, God's hand of protection, mercy, and restoration is hindered at best and stopped at worst."
- *The Integrated Approach To Biblical Healing Ministry* by Chester and Betsy Kystra

"When an individual wrongs you, it is very easy to hold bitterness, resentment, anger and unforgiveness. However, this works against your body and will eventually cause disease to set in. It is far better for your body - for both your mental and physical health – to forgive the person and release these deadly emotions before they take root in your mind and body. The Bible says it plainly: "Do not let the sun go down on your anger" (Eph 4:26, NAS). This, I believe, is one of the most important keys in preventing these emotions from locking onto our minds and bodies and eventually killing us."
- *The Bible Cure For Depression and Anxiety* by Don Colbert, M.D.

Matthew 5:22a (AMP)
"But I say to you that anyone that continues to be angry with his brother or harbors malice (enmity of the heart) against him shall be liable to *and* unable to escape the punishment imposed by the court;"

Author's Note: Unforgiveness is extremely costly!

Unforgiveness Will Hinder and Prevent Healing, Invite Sickness and Open the Door to Demonic Oppression

Matthew 5:25-26
"**Settle matters *(forgive)* quickly** with your adversary who is taking you to court. Do it quickly while you are still on the way, or he may hand you over to the judge, and the judge may hand you over to the officer, and you will be thrown into prison. I tell you the truth, you will not get out until you have paid the last penny."

Author's Note: "Settle matters quickly (forgive matters quickly) with your adversary" or be "throw into prison" until you do forgive him.

Matthew 18:32-35 (AMP)
Then the master called him and said to him, "You contemptible *and* wicked attendant! I forgave *and* cancelled all that [great] debt of yours because you begged me to. And should you not have had pity *and* mercy on your fellow attendant, as I have had on you?" And in wrath his master turned him over to the torturers (the jailers), till he should pay all he owed. So also my heavenly Father will deal with every one of you **if you do not freely forgive your brother from your heart** *his offenses*.

Author's Note: Unforgiveness opens the door to the torturers (demonic oppression) resulting in mental and emotion torture and sickness.

Mark 11:24-26 (AMP)
"For this reason I am telling you, whatever you ask for in prayer, believe (trust and be confident) that it is granted to you, and you will [get it]. And whenever you stand praying, if you have anything against anyone, **forgive him *and* let it drop** (leave it, let it go), in order that your Father who is in heaven may also forgive you your failings *and* short comings

Unforgiveness Will Hinder and Prevent Healing, Invite Sickness and Open the Door to Demonic Oppression

and let them drop. But if you do not forgive, neither will your Father in heaven forgive your failings and shortcomings."

Note by Chester and Betsy Kystra: "That is enough for me, knowing that if I don't forgive, He's not going to forgive me. I'm not willing to pay the price of not having Him forgive me, of being out from under His protection, or of being turned over to the tormentors. I'm willing to do whatever it takes."
- *The Integrated Approach to Biblical Healing Ministry*

Luke 6:37 (AMP)
Judge not [neither pronouncing judgment nor subjecting to censure], and you will not be judged; do not condemn *and* pronounce guilty, and you will not be condemned *and* pronounced guilty; acquit *and* forgive *and* release (give up resentment, let it drop), and you will be acquitted *and* forgiven *and* released.

Luke 6:38
"Give, and it will be given to you. A good measure, pressed down, shaken together and running over, will be poured into your lap. For with the measure you use, it will be measured to you."

Note by Chester and Betsy Kystra: "When applied in a godly way, this (giving) principle has very positive results. If, however, we apply it negatively, giving to others seeds of bitterness or hatred or anger or violence or rage or abuse, watch out! If we give away these types of "seed," then that's what we can expect in return. The amount will be "full measure, pressed down, shaken together, running over." - *The Integrated Approach to Biblical Healing Ministry*

Unforgiveness Will Hinder and Prevent Healing, Invite Sickness and Open the Door to Demonic Oppression

2 Corinthians 2:10-11
it you forgive anyone, I will also forgive him. And what I have forgiven – if there was anything to forgive – I have forgiven in sight of Christ for your sake, **in order that Satan might not outwit us**. For we are not unaware of his schemes.

Author's Note: Satan's scheme is to keep you in unforgiveness, which gives him the legal right and free access to torment and oppress you.

Galatians 6:7
Do not be deceived: God cannot be mocked. A man reaps what he sows.

Author's Note: If a man sows unforgiveness, he will reap the fruit of unforgiveness: mental and emotional torture and sickness.

54
Cursing Yourself with Sickness Through Word Curses

The Ungodly Things You Speak Towards Yourself or Your Health Condition Can Prevent Healing and Bring Sickness and Trouble to Your Life

"When you confess lack of faith your doubt increases. Every time you confess doubts and fears, you confess your faith in Satan and deny the ability and the grace of God. When you confess doubt, you are imprisoned with your own words. Proverbs 6:2, "You have been trapped by what you said, ensnared by the words of your mouth." When we doubt His Word it is because we believe something else that is contrary to that Word. Wrong confession shuts the Father out and lets Satan in."
- *Christ The Healer* by F.F. Bosworth

Job 15:6
Your own mouth condemns you, not mine; your own lips testify against you.

Psalm 59:12
For the sins of their mouths, for the words of their lips, **let them be caught** in their pride. For the curses and lies they utter,

Author's Note: Any word we speak about our health condition that is contrary to God's Word is a lie and puts us in danger of being "caught" and cursed by that lie.

Psalm 64:8
He will turn their own tongues against them and bring them to ruin; all who see them will shake their heads in scorn.

Cursing Yourself with Sickness Through Word Curses

Psalm 109:17-20
He loved to pronounce a curse – may it come on him; he found no pleasure in blessing - may it be far from him. He wore cursing as his garment; it entered his body like water, into his bones like oil.

Psalm 140:9
Let the heads of those who surround me be covered with the **trouble their lips have caused**.

Proverbs 6:2-3
If you have been trapped by what you said, **ensnared by the words of your mouth**, then do this, my son, to free yourself …Go and humble yourself, press your plea …

Author's Note: "To free yourself" get humble before God and ask Him to forgive you of any words you confessed that are contrary to His Word. And then ask Him to help you stay free from confessing words that will ensnare your life.

Proverbs 12:13
An evil man is **trapped by his sinful talk**, but a righteous man escapes trouble.

Proverbs 13:3
He who guards his lips guards his life, but **he who speaks rashly will come to ruin.**

Proverbs 17:20
A man of perverse heart does not prosper; he whose tongue is deceitful falls into trouble.

Author's Note: We will fall into trouble if our confession regarding our health circumstance is contrary (deceitful) to the healing promises of God.

Cursing Yourself with Sickness Through Word Curses

Proverbs 18:7a
A fool's mouth is his undoing,

Proverbs 18:21 (AMP)
Death and life are in the power of the tongue, and they who indulge in it shall eat the fruit of it [for death or life].

Proverbs 21:23
He who guards his mouth and his tongue keeps himself from calamity.

Ecclesiastes 10:12
Words of a wise man's mouth are gracious, but a fool is consumed by his own lips.

Matthew 12:37
"For by your words you will be acquitted, and by your words you will be condemned."

Matthew 15:10-11
Jesus called the crowd to Him and said, "Listen and understand. What goes into a man's mouth does not make him 'unclean,' but **what comes out of his mouth**, that is what makes him 'unclean.'"

Mark 11:21
Peter remembered and said to Jesus, "Rabbi, look! The fig tree you cursed has withered!"

Author's Note: Be careful not to curse your own body or health situation. It can be your undoing and make you "withered" in your health.

Cursing Yourself with Sickness Through Word Curses

James 3:6
The tongue is also a fire, a world of evil among the parts of the body. **It corrupts the whole person, sets the whole course of his life** on fire, and is itself set on fire by hell.

Author's Note: Your own tongue can "corrupt" your health.

James 3:9-10
With the tongue we praise our Lord and Father, and **with it we curse men** *(and ourselves)*, who have been made in God's likeness. Out of the same mouth come praise and cursing. My brothers, this should not be.

Authors Note: You can curse yourself with sickness by your own words.

1 Peter 3:10
For, "Whoever would love life and see good days must keep his tongue from evil and his lips from deceitful speech."

Recommended Reading:
- *The Final Quest* by Rick Joyner
- *God's Covenant Of Healing* by S.J. Hill
- *Christ The Healer* by F.F. Bosworth
- *Open my eyes Lord'* by Gary Oats
- *The Bible Cure For Depression and Anxiety* by Don Colbert, M.D.
- *The Integrated Approach to Biblical Healing* by Chester and Betsy Kystra
- Sid Roth's Messianic Vision Radio Show - www.sidroth.org

Special thanks to my incredible wife Dara for her grace, help, and shared vision. Thank you Jesus and Glory to God!

The Bible Healing Promise Book

To order toll-free: (866) 909-BOOK

Order online at: www.xulonpress.com

www.biblehealingbook.com

CPSIA information can be obtained at www.ICGtesting.com
Printed in the USA
LVOW091228100812

293775LV00002B/173/A